# GOD'S ICEBREAKER

# GOD'S ICEBREAKER

## The Life and Adventures
## of Father Ted Hesburgh of Notre Dame

by

Jill A. Boughton
and
Julie Walters

GOD'S ICEBREAKER:
the Life and Adventures of
Father Ted Hesburgh of Notre Dame

10 9 8 7 6 5 4 3

ISBN 978-0-9833586-6-4

Published by
**Corby Books**
A Division of Corby Publishing LP
P.O. Box 93
Notre Dame, Indiana 46556
(574) 784-3482
www.corbypublishing.com

Distributed by
ACTA Publications
4848 N. Clark Street, Chicago, IL 60640 ~ 800-397-2282 ~ www.actapublications.com

Manufactured in the United States of America

# In Gratitude

We are grateful to Rev. Ted Hesburgh, C.S.C., for granting us an interview and listening to a version of our introductory chapter. Obviously we have relied on the information in his autobiography *God, Country, Notre Dame,* his *Travels with Ted and Ned* and the well- researched, *Hesburgh: A Biography* by Michael O'Brien. But we have also invented dialogue to liven up the story for young readers.

Charles Lamb of the University of Notre Dame Archives and Rev. Christopher Kuhn, C.S.C., of the Indiana Province Archives Center, were very helpful in locating photographs to illustrate the book. We have also used one photo from Father Ted's personal collection.

Those who have worked with Father Ted in recent years also provided helpful information and stories, including Melanie Chapleau, Rev. Austin Collins, C.S.C., Rev. Paul Doyle, C.S.C., and Rev. Charles Lavely, C.S.C.

For the form of the ordination ceremony used in 1943, we consulted Rev. Bob Pelton, C.S.C., and Rev. George Gabet, F.S.S.P. Rev. Raymond Willy and Tony Sands of Family Theater Productions who got us a copy of their documentary on Father Ted.

We are grateful to Jennifer Conlan and Gerry Goggins, and to our families, for believing in this project.

# Table of Contents

Chapter One

# Hooked for Life

F ROM THE HELICOPTER WINDOW, the priest watched the icebreaker working below. As it rammed a field of ice sixteen feet thick, large chunks fell into the seas of Antarctica. The icebreaker backed up one thousand feet into a cleared ribbon of water and surged forward again. It reminded him of a bucking bronco at a rodeo.

As the helicopter descended, the priest grabbed the seat and held on. The deck of the bucking ship seemed an impossible target, and it felt as if everything was in slow motion. "Come, Holy Spirit," he prayed. Then the pilot dropped the helicopter onto the tiny landing pad, and suddenly it was over. How could he have ever imagined his life as a priest might be dull?

"You made it," a sailor said as he helped the priest out of the chopper.

"By the grace of God," he said. Then he looked back over his shoulder, "—and a terrific pilot."

The year was 1963. The priest was Father Theodore M. Hesburgh, C.S.C., President of the University of Notre Dame. That Sunday morning, Father Hesburgh was on assignment with the National Science Board. But wherever he went, whatever job he had, Father Ted was first and foremost a priest.

It was fitting for Father Ted to be on an icebreaker because he acted as an icebreaker on many occasions. With the prayer "Come, Holy Spirit" on his lips, he led the way in breaking down many barriers. He broke through icy relationships between the United States and Russia during the Cold War. He broke down deep-seated prejudices that denied rights to African-Americans, women, and lay Catholics. As the president of Notre Dame, he broke up a mob of college students so angry about the war in Vietnam that they planned to burn down a building. At the age of sixty-one, he even broke a speed record in an SR-71 Blackbird spy jet piloted by Major Tom Allison.

The sailor smiled. "Welcome aboard the *Eastwind*, Father. This is great. We haven't seen a priest since we left Rhode Island six weeks ago."

"Well, we'll make up for that today," said Father Ted, following the sailor down a metal flight of steps and through a narrow hallway.

The sailor opened a door to a tiny room. "Father, I hope this cabin will do. It's all we have free at the moment."

"This is fine," Father Ted said, unzipping his parka. "In ten minutes I'll be ready to hear confessions."

"I'm sorry the captain didn't slow down for you," said the sailor. "He's clearing the way for two tankers. McMurdo Sound Station is in dire need of their oil. Our captain takes his job very seriously, and he won't let anything or anyone interfere."

"I understand," said Father Ted. "I admire a man who takes his job seriously. Do we have time for Mass before breakfast?"

"You bet, Father. I'll alert the Catholics. How about Mass five minutes after you hear the last confession?"

"Perfect timing."

Father Ted opened his portable Mass kit. He laid a linen cloth on the table and put a small crucifix and candles on it. He even had a tiny altar stone for the altar table. He unpacked cruets of wine and water, a chalice to hold the wine, and a paten for the communion bread. Simple preparations completed, he put on the stole that marked him as a priest and opened the door.

Father Ted loved to hear confessions because he could bring Christ's forgiveness to people and help them find practical ways to change their lives. After he heard the last man's confession, the priest asked him to tell the others it was time for Mass.

Father Ted greeted each young man as he walked through the door. Then he began the Mass: "*In nomine Patris, et Filii, et Spiritus Sancti*" ["In the name of the Father, and of the Son, and of the Holy Spirit"]. In 1963 the Mass was still celebrated in Latin everywhere in the world, but that was soon to change. Catholic Church leaders were meeting in Rome at the Second Vatican Council, where they would decide that the Mass could be celebrated in the native language of each country.

"Amen," the men answered.

As Father Ted continued with the Mass, he leaned one way then another to keep his footing. He consecrated the communion wafers with Christ's words "*Hoc est enim Corpus meum*" ["This is my Body"]. These words made Christ truly present—even though the host looked the same as it had before. With reverence, Father Ted held up the host so all the men could see it.

As he put the communion wafer on each man's tongue,

Father Ted felt privileged to be nourishing men who were so hungry for Christ.

After Mass he followed the men to the mess hall and went through the food line. "What a breakfast! This should keep me going all day," he said as he sat down at the table.

Father Ted's pilot told the sailors, "He'll need it. He's only had four hours of sleep, and he's scheduled to say two more Masses, one at the South Pole and one a half continent away at Byrd Station."

Father Ted smiled at a sailor with a Southern accent. "How do you like all this ice and snow?" he asked. The young man shrugged his shoulders.

Father Ted said, "Snow always makes me think of Father Sorin, the first president of Notre Dame. He came from the milder climate of France. When he arrived at what is now the University of Notre Dame in 1842, it was winter. He looked out across the frozen lake and put his mission into Our Lady's hands.

"I hope some of you gentlemen will come see me at Notre Dame. It's a beautiful campus and a wonderful place to study and pray. Perhaps God has even tapped one or two of you to become priests.

"But I've talked enough. Tell me about the work of the *Eastwind.*"

"*Eastwind* is a great icebreaker," a young sailor proudly explained. "She participated in Deep Freeze I in 1955 to '56 to help get ready for the International Geophysical Year. In 1957 and '58, forty nations collaborated on earth science studies all over the globe. *Eastwind* has continued to be involved in research, resupplying military bases, and breaking ice to free trapped vessels. Two years ago, she was the first cutter to circumnavigate the globe."

Another man said, "Admiral Byrd was part of Deep Freeze I. He traveled all over Antarctica."

"I'm privileged to be aboard. You do vital work." Father Ted reached into his pocket and pulled out rosaries and Notre Dame medals. As he handed them out, he promised, "I'll pray my rosary for you and your captain. And I hope to see you again on my turf."

\* \* \*

"This is a great flight for me," Father Ted told the pilot on the helicopter's sixty-mile return trip. "As a teenager, I read the adventures of Robert Falcon Scott, the polar explorer. That must be the hut where he lived in 1910!"

As they flew over a peak, the pilot pointed. "That's Mount Erebus on your right. It's still an active volcano."

A little while later, Father Ted asked, "Is that Cape Crozier? It's such a clear day, I think I can see penguins down there."

"Yes, it is. You know your geography, Father."

Back at the station, Father Ted and the pilot stopped at a bust of Admiral Byrd with a plaque that read:

*Richard Evelyn Bird,*
*Rear Admiral United States Navy.*
*October 25, 1888–March 11, 1957*

*"I am hopeful that Antarctica in its symbolic robe of white will shine forth as a continent of peace as nations working together there in the cause of science will set an example of international peace."*

*To all who follow in Admiral Byrd's footsteps*
*This monument is dedicated*
*The National Geographic Society*

As they continued walking, Father Ted said, "Admiral Byrd was a brave man—and so are you. You executed that tricky landing beautifully."

"Thank you, Father. It's been good to be with you," the pilot said.

Father Ted transferred to a plane headed to the South Pole. The plane was carrying fifteen hundred pounds of TNT to be used to shake the landscape in order to study it. Father Ted knew that if anything went wrong, they would be blown to smithereens. He was at peace with God, but he hoped this wouldn't be his last flight. He was only forty-six years old, and he believed that he still had much to do.

As soon as the plane was airborne, Father Ted began chatting with pilot Larry Gould, "I heard you were Admiral Byrd's executive officer and pilot."

"Yes, I was part of the American expedition in 1928. Admiral Byrd's goal was to fly over the South Pole. He named me second in command. I'm also a geologist, so I helped with exploration and research projects."

"What kind of man was Admiral Byrd?" Father Ted asked.

"Let me tell you a story. Two other pilots and I flew out on a survey flight. We landed 140 miles from Little America. Then a ferocious blizzard came up and destroyed our plane. It also knocked out our radios. As soon as the weather cleared, a search plane found us, and the Admiral himself flew out to rescue us. The pilot who brought him told me that as soon as they landed, he got down on his knees and prayed. He was so grateful to see the three of us alive and hardy."

"It's wonderful to know he was a man of prayer," said Father Ted.

"He was quite a man," Larry continued, "but he did fail

in one endeavor that meant a lot to him. In 1927, Admiral Byrd was one of many aviators who attempted the first nonstop flight between the United States and France. His plane crashed. Neither he nor his pilot had serious injuries, but while the plane was being repaired, Charles Lindbergh beat him to the prize."

"I remember that!" exclaimed Father Ted. "It was 1927, and I was ten. I fell in love with flying that summer. I was at the parade honoring Lindy on his return to New York! I had attended my cousin's ordination to the priesthood at St. Patrick's Cathedral. I watched and listened to every word because I already knew I wanted to be a priest.

"Afterward I ran outside and wiggled through the crowd until I found myself standing in tickertape up to my knees. Lindbergh was the first man to make a solo flight across the Atlantic from New York to Paris—and I was there to see him return victorious! I was one awestruck ten-year-old. I yelled and waved until my arms hurt.

"That same summer my friend Eddie Naughton helped me build one model airplane after another. When we heard about a daredevil pilot performing stunts at a nearby airport, we begged our dads to take us.

"The pilot was dressed in a helmet, goggles, leather jacket, white scarf, flared cavalry pants, and high-laced boots."

"He sounds like a real barnstormer," said Larry.

"Yes he was, and he was giving rides for five dollars a person. That was a lot of money in 1927, but we begged so hard that our dads forked over the money. Boy, were we excited when we boarded that creaky biplane. It had a wooden propeller. The pilot belted us in the front seat then stepped over us to take his seat in back.

"It was amazing to see the farms and woods and cars

and people below us. From the open cockpit, I could see downtown Syracuse and Lake Onondaga. After that fifteen-minute ride, I was hooked for life."

As Father Ted was finishing his story, they approached the landing strip. Larry lined the plane up between the oil drums that marked the ten-thousand-foot runway. Just as they were about to touch down, they hit something. They bounced back up, and the plane veered sharply to the left. Larry cut power to the two left engines, revved up the right ones, and dropped in for a perfect landing.

"Whew!" Father Ted exhaled. "That was one of the most beautiful pieces of airmanship I have ever seen. I was sure we were going to crash." He later learned they had hit a *sastrugi*, an icy spike that is formed by the wind.

The men at the station were all busy, so Father Ted's scheduled Mass was postponed. "Are you up for the mile walk to the South Pole?" Larry asked. "I've been to Antarctica four times, but I've never actually seen the Pole."

"Let's go," said Father Ted, pulling his hood close around his face.

As they trudged through the whiteness, Larry whispered, "I feel as if I'm on a religious pilgrimage. Would you mind if we kept silence?"

Father Ted agreed. He prayed quietly as they walked.

When they arrived at the southernmost spot in the world, they found it was marked simply. Nothing was there but a flagpole supported by guy wires. As visitors to this remote spot always do, Father Ted and Larry walked all the way around the guy wires. In covering the 360 degrees of this circle, they crossed every line of the earth's longitude. So it took them about sixty seconds to travel around the world!

Father Ted breathed a short prayer and felt like a priest for the whole world.

### Chapter Two

# God Has Other Plans for Me

I T WAS THE KIND OF cold winter day Ted loved. A bright sun was shining in a blue, blue sky, and snow coated every tree and bush like whipped cream. A stiff wind was blowing at his back. Ted stretched out his arms and skated across the slick ice on Onondaga Park's skating rink.

Nine-year-old Betty must have been watching. Out of the corner of his eye, Ted saw her hold out her arms and sail too. But she soon bumped into a teenage boy.

After two hours, Ted caught Betty's eye. He held up one finger and pointed to the exit, signaling, "One more round, then we have to go." He skated backward toward the exit. By the time he sat on the snow-crusted ground to take off his skates, he was experiencing that sense of calm that sets in after strenuous exercise.

Ted's head was down and his fingers were stiff as he tried to untie the thick laces. He was thinking of a cup of hot chocolate in a warm kitchen when suddenly he heard bells jingling behind him. He looked over his shoulder.

Spiked-shoed horses were pulling a sleigh straight toward him! No time to jump out of the way. Ted flattened his body face down in the snow. He felt the ground tremble as the horses passed on either side of his prone body. A second later, the runners of the sleigh flashed by, as well.

He felt the cold on his cheek. He heard the bells fade away. Ted lay still. Nothing hurt. He was alive. Untouched. He was alive, and he knew why. Trembling, he sat up. His sister hurried to his side.

"You could have been killed," someone gasped.

The words came out before he had time to think. "Oh, no," Ted said, "God has other plans for me."

People crowded around him. Someone said, "It was a miracle."

Ted thanked the bystanders, turned down a ride home, and walked away from the park. He always walked quickly, so Betty had to run to keep up.

"What plans does God have for you?" she asked.

Ted's mind flashed back to the decision he made when he was six. From that point on, he knew God wanted him to be a priest. As a priest he could do great good for many of the people he would meet.

Ted didn't answer Betty's question. "I don't want to talk about it right now. Let's get home. Think you can keep up with me?"

"Yep!"

As they walked into the kitchen, Betty yelled, "Ted was almost killed by horses and a sleigh."

Ted's mother hugged him then looked into his eyes for evidence of a concussion.

His father took him by both shoulders. "Are you all right, son? Your right cheek is pretty red. You might have a nasty bruise there."

"He was almost killed. Somebody said so," Betty repeated.

Ted elbowed Betty with his eyes and she looked down.

"I'm okay," said Ted. "Really, I'm okay. Just a little shook up."

"Here, Ted, this will warm you up." Mrs. Hesburgh poured hot chocolate into cups and passed them out. She brought out a plate of sugar cookies, and everyone sat around the kitchen table while Ted told them what happened.

Mr. Hesburgh said, "We'll devote tomorrow's rosary to thanking God and the Blessed Mother for Ted's safety."

* * *

Theodore Martin Hesburgh was born on Friday, May 25, 1917, in Syracuse, New York, and baptized at St. Anthony's Church. A short time later Anne Marie Murphy Hesburgh wrote in his baby book: "Mother was so glad God sent her a little boy, for sister would be so glad when she grew up to have a brother. Daddy was so happy his face looked like a morning in June."

Always called Ted, he was the third Theodore Hesburgh. But instead of being Theodore Bernard like his father and grandfather, Ted got his middle name from his other grandfather, Martin Murphy.

In the early days the Hesburghs lived in apartments. There Ted and his sisters had to play quietly to avoid disturbing the people who lived over them or under them. Then one day his father took the family to see their newly built house in the suburb of Strathmore. Breathing in the scent of fresh new wood, Ted followed his father through the house.

Even at eight, Ted knew how long and hard his father had worked to buy that new house for his family. After church every Sunday, his Dad went into the office to organize things for the following week's work. He had recently been named manager of the Pittsburgh Plate Glass Company's new Syracuse store. Now he wouldn't have to travel five days a week to cover his upstate New York sales region. He had landed a job with that company right out of high school, the youngest man to be given a new territory. At first he drove a horse and buggy, and then he traded them for a Model T Ford.

Ted heard a story about one of his Dad's early sales. A resistant hardware store owner was about to throw his father out when Mr. Hesburgh spotted a picture of Theodore Roosevelt on the wall. "This is a great man," he said.

"What do you know about Colonel Roosevelt?" the owner challenged.

Perhaps because they shared the same first name, Theodore Hesburgh knew plenty about the former President. He talked at length about the charge up San Juan Hill and other Roosevelt exploits. Before he left the store, he had bagged his biggest sale of the week.

At home Ted watched his father work just as hard transplanting bushes and trees from the woods behind the house to landscape their lawn. While his father maneuvered a wheelbarrow and shovel, Ted and his neighborhood buddies built a tree fort in those woods.

Ted loved his summer activities. At Boy Scout camp he worked hard to earn as many badges as possible. He joined a neighborhood softball team that played in a vacant lot down the block. Ted wasn't a very good batter or outfielder, but the team kept encouraging him when he made mistakes.

Ted's favorite part of the summer was a two-week vacation at a cottage on Lake Ontario. Before every outing, he and his sisters scrambled to get their rosaries. They knew Dad would lead the family rosary as soon as they got settled in the car.

The first day at the cottage, Ted plunged into the cold lake and swam a few yards. Mary put in a toe, then her foot. Her little sisters followed timidly. They eased in up to their knees, giggling and shivering with every step.

Ted learned to fish as a young boy on those summer outings. Before long he was catching enough fish for the family's

Friday dinners. In the Catholic Church at that time, Fridays were days of abstinence when Catholics were not allowed to eat meat.

In the fall Ted was a lineman for the Robineau Terriers, a neighborhood football team. As a second stringer, he had to borrow a leather helmet from a starter when he was subbed into the game.

Morning rain on the day the Terriers were scheduled to play their rivals from Rochester filled the field with mud. From the sidelines Ted watched both teams slip and slide, fumbling one ball after another.

When his team was ahead 25-0, Ted's coach finally put in the second team. Ted took his teammate's rain-soaked helmet. Fastening it clumsily, he sloshed onto the field. He was twice as tall as the opposing Allendale lineman, but Ted's opponent threw his whole body into blocking. After pushing hard against each other, they both landed on the muddy ground after every play.

When Ted walked through the kitchen door, he could hear his mother singing. She took one look at her mud-spattered son and said in her best Irish brogue, "Teddy, you look like Paddy's Pig that's enjoyed himself wallowing in a mud hole."

They both laughed, "Go on down to the basement, Ted. Put that awful uniform on the floor in front of the washing machine. I'll get your bathrobe, so you can go upstairs and take a bath." She turned back to give the pot on the stove a stir.

"Did your team win?"

Ted grinned. "Yep! 25-0. And I got to play the last part of the game."

"I'm glad. You deserve a chance, after showing up for every practice."

Ted nodded. "Well, you always say I shouldn't have my nose stuck in a book all the time."

But Ted did love to read. One winter Saturday evening, he lay down by the fireplace to read Edison Marshall, one of his favorite authors. Marshall's adventure tales spanned the globe, from Arctic snow to the African jungle.

As usual, his father was in his favorite chair reading the newspaper.

"No baseball stats to follow this time of year, huh, Dad?" Ted commented.

"No. Sometimes I wish the New York Yankees and the Brooklyn Dodgers played all year round. It looks like this year there will be no New York Celtics basketball games either. Fans just don't have the money in these tough times to spend on basketball tickets."

Mr. Hesburgh folded the paper to the crossword puzzle. "Think I'll tackle this now, and then get back to my book," he said, picking up a pencil and his well-thumbed dictionary.

Ted looked into the yellow, orange, red, and blue flames. His father was a man who spoke few words, but he always managed to beat Ted at word games. Although he didn't express affection, he showed his love for his family by working hard to provide for them.

On visits to his Great Aunt Mary, Ted learned that his Dad had a tough start in life. Ted's Grandfather Hesburgh was a schoolteacher, who had a happy marriage until tragedy struck his young family. Within two weeks, his wife and two of his three young sons died. Heart-broken, Grandfather Hesburgh left the Catholic Church and his job in New York City. He took his three-year-old son—Ted's father—to live with relatives on an Iowa corn farm.

Aunt Mary sensed that her nephew needed a woman's guiding hand. She took a train to Iowa, brought Ted's father back to Staten Island, and raised him as her own. During high school, he worked as a pinsetter in a bowling alley during the day and attended classes at night. Even at that age, he had to be serious about work and his education.

When Ted was old enough to make the long trip to Brooklyn by himself, he began hearing Grandfather Hesburgh's own stories. Although his ancestors were German, he had also taught himself English, Yiddish, Russian, French, Italian, and Spanish, so he could pay his way through college selling patent medicines door-to-door to New Yorkers who spoke those languages.

Ted's mother sat down in her chair on the other side of the fire with her mending basket.

"No singing tonight, Mom?" asked Ted wistfully.

"Not tonight, Ted," she answered. "If I don't patch these pants, you won't have anything to wear to school Monday. Dad has two buttons missing on his shirt, and I have to let Mary's and Betty's uniform skirts down. Thank the good Lord Anne isn't having a growth spurt now."

On most Saturday evenings his mother played the piano, and the children sang Irish songs with her. Even tonight he could hear her humming as she worked. Her affection and ready laughter balanced his father's serious approach to life. Ted knew his mother missed being able to go to plays and concerts in New York City, but his father was glad to live far from the city's noise and dirt.

Ted also loved listening to his mother's stories. She told him about Grandfather Martin Murphy, a fun-loving Irish plumber who went to 6 a.m. Mass with his wife every morning. After the difficult birth of their only child, Anne's mother was confined to a wheelchair. Anne was only ten when she died.

After taking business courses in high school, Ted's mother worked as a secretary for an AT&T executive. She spent her free time with a lively group of young people at picnics on the Hudson River and parties in the City. There she met Theodore Hesburgh. It wasn't long before he was traveling every weekend from upstate New York to the Bronx to visit her.

About the time they were getting serious about each other, Anne Marie Murphy entered a contest at the Metropolitan Opera. Her lovely soprano voice won her a scholarship to La Scala Opera in Milan, Italy. Theodore was crestfallen. He didn't want to stand in her way, but he was afraid he'd never see her again. What if she went off and married some Italian? Instead of sailing for Italy, Anne turned down the scholarship and married her handsome 6'2" salesman. After their 1913 wedding in the Bronx, they moved to Syracuse, New York.

Ted wasn't surprised at his mother's choice. He could see how much his parents loved one another. They taught their children to be honest, to work hard, to be loyal to their country and the Catholic Church. The children knew who was in charge and tried never to disappoint their parents.

After school one day, Ted yelled, "I'm home," dropped his books on the kitchen table and barged into the living room. He found his mother comforting a weeping neighbor. Embarrassed, Ted backed into the kitchen and made himself a peanut butter sandwich.

When the neighbor left, Ted's mother told him she had come to say goodbye to her only friend in the neighborhood. In the two or three years she lived in Strathmore, Ted's mother had been the only person who spoke to her. Finally she couldn't stand it any longer; she decided to move.

Ted didn't understand. "Why won't the neighbors speak to her?"

"She's Jewish," his mother replied.

"So what?" Ted persisted. O'Brien p.10)

His mother explained that there were few Catholics and no other Jews in their segregated neighborhood. She said Catholics were tolerated because they had a little money, otherwise they would not be welcome either.

That day, an indignant Ted learned how hurtful prejudice was.

In seventh grade, Ted won first prize in a New York State geography contest. How he itched to find out "what was over the next hill"! He read book after book: adventure, romance, travel, and biographies of brave Christians who lived and died for their faith.

When Ted was an eighth grade altar boy, four mission-aries from the Congregation of Holy Cross came to preach "fire and brimstone sermons." The boys who served Mass were considered too young to hear this, so one of the visitors took them aside to tell them about life as a Holy Cross priest. Ted really liked Father Tom Duffy. He seemed like a great priest.

And Father Duffy was impressed with Ted. "A fine boy, bright," he noted on a scrap of paper. He asked Ted what he wanted to do when he grew up. Ted replied. "I'm going to be a priest, Father, like you." (O'Brien p. 11)

Hoping Ted truly had a vocation—a call from God to become a priest—Father Duffy visited the Hesburgh home. Ted listened closely as Father Duffy talked to his parents. He sat quietly wondering when and how his life was going to change.

Father Duffy urged Ted's parents to send him to high school seminary at the University of Notre Dame in South Bend, Indiana.

Ted knew God wanted him to be a priest, and he liked what he'd heard about the Holy Cross Order. They had missionary priests, and the adventuresome life of a foreign missionary appealed to Ted. But was he ready to leave his family? Could he live so far away from them?

Although Ted's mother approved of his desire to be a priest, she thought thirteen was too young to leave home. "No dice, Father Duffy," she said.

"If he goes to high school here, he may lose his vocation," Father Duffy warned.

Ted's mother looked the priest straight in the eye and said, "It can't be much of a vocation if he's going to lose it by living in a Christian family."

Mother had spoken and that was that.

Chapter Three

# Something More

I T WAS 2 A.M. BY THE TIME TED got home from the dance. He had had a great time with his friends. But as he sat on the edge of his bed to take off his shoes, he realized once again that there was something missing in his life.

He put on his pajamas slowly, thoughtfully, then slipped under the covers. As he turned on his side, he smiled to himself. Yes, he definitely wanted more out of life.

Ted had a priest friend who regularly heard his confessions and knew Ted intended to become a priest. "Father, should I be going to dances?" Ted asked him. "Is it right for me to go to parties, or should I be getting ready for the seminary by staying home and praying?"

Father chuckled. "You need to lead a normal high school social life. Go ahead and date. Have fun," he said. "Just don't do anything you'll be ashamed of when you become a priest." (O'Brien p. 18)

Ted was a little surprised, but he liked that advice, so he socialized as much as everyone else. He just kept the priest's admonition in mind. Since their school didn't organize many social events, a group of boys and girls planned picnics, parties, and swimming outings.

One summer afternoon a group of friends went swimming in Lake Onondaga. One of the guys splashed Ted and said admiringly, "Hey, someone said you look like a cross between Tyrone Power and Fredric March."

"Those movie stars?" shrugged Ted, unconsciously smoothing his black curly hair. "Nope, I get my good looks from my Irish and German ancestors."

Ted often asked Mary Eleanor Kelley to dance with him. She was a great dancer, lively and attractive as well. They bantered easily, trading quips. No matter who won the exchange, they both ended up laughing. Friends whispered that they were sweet on each other. Some wondered if Mary Eleanor might make Ted change his mind about becoming a priest. But Ted never wavered.

Ted and his friends went to high school football, basketball, and baseball games. Ted joined his friends in cheering on the teams, but he never went out for a sport in high school.

Besides going to school and going to parties, Ted had to earn money to help his family. The country was in the Depression. Jobs were scarce, and wages were low. Ted scrounged to earn money. He mowed lawns and hauled coal ashes. He combed the woods for watercress and nuts, then sold them door to door.

Ted also sold newspapers. Since there was no TV, people relied on special issues of the paper to keep up with important events that happened between regular issues. Waving a newspaper overhead, Ted would shout, "Extra! Extra!" These "extras" put extra money in Ted's pocket.

During his senior year of high school, Ted worked forty hours a week at a gas station, getting grease under his fingernails and learning a little more about cars. This came in handy when Ted and his buddies decided to scrape together enough money to buy a run-down Model T Ford. Ted's boss gave them tips on how to keep the car running, but they often ended up with grease all over them. When the car did run, they went as far as the other side of town to visit friends, but they always carried tools in case it broke down.

The guys couldn't trust their car for longer trips. When they fished for bass on a lake in the Adirondacks or hunted pheasant near Rochester, New York, they borrowed a family car. Once they headed off to a cabin on a lake for the whole weekend. Two days with no jobs or schoolwork!

The first thing they unpacked was a big block of ice wrapped in a blanket; the cabin didn't have a modern refrigerator, only an icebox cooled by ice placed in the top compartment.

"Don't forget the cigars in the back seat," Ted said over his shoulder as he hefted a basket of food their mothers had packed. "We won't starve this weekend," he said. "This is enough food for a month."

After unpacking their duffel bags and cleaning their rifles, they ate lunch and then spent the rest of the day hunting. They were able to bag two pheasants, which they dressed and cooked for supper. That night they stayed up playing poker, smoking cigars, and feeling grown up.

The next morning they got up before dawn and caught enough bass for breakfast. They put the fish on ice while they went to Mass at a small church in the nearest town. They had time to hunt again that afternoon before they headed home. Taking a final look around the cabin to make sure they had everything, one of Ted's buddies said, "This is the life! I wish we could stay forever."

It was his love of hunting that sent Ted to the principal's office for the only time in his high school career. He skipped school on the first day of pheasant-hunting season. To his embarrassment, his parents were called into the principal's office with him. He was sorry he had caused them this humiliation.

"Only vulgar people go hunting," the principal said emphatically. A picture of former President Theodore Roosevelt hunting big game flashed into Ted's mind, but he was smart enough to keep his mouth shut. He didn't intend to see the inside of Sister-Principal's office ever again!

Although Ted had a great sense of humor, he didn't participate in schoolboy pranks. He didn't clash with teachers or other students, and he worked hard at his studies. Every day for twelve years he buttoned up a clean white shirt and pulled on blue dress pants. He walked the mile to and from Most Holy Rosary School in all kinds of weather. In high school he took four years of English, Latin, and religion; three years of French and history; and one year each of algebra, geometry, and chemistry. He also studied government, art, and drama.

Ted joined the high school's Literary Guild, whose members each delivered oral book reviews. In March 1934, he reported on the biography *Father McShane of Maryknoll*. Father McShane was a missionary in South China. He rescued an abandoned Chinese baby—then caught smallpox from the child and died.

Ted read the author's conclusion, "We need men who are as pure of heart, who are truly humble, whose motives are single, whose courage is marked, who are fearless in the charity of Christ." Ted could see that his realistic report enthralled his fellow guild members.

His senior year, Ted helped edit *The Rosarian*, the school newspaper. In one of his articles, he urged his fellow students to give up the "dime novel," where the hero kills the "big bad bandit, marries the foreman's daughter, and lives bloodily ever after." Instead, they should read "GOOD books." Books that were "true to life, interesting, and would satiate your most sanguinary tastes, elevate your ideas, enlarge your vocabulary, and widen your perspective." He recommended nine specific books in three categories: travel, adventure and religion.

One of the books Ted recommended was *Mush, You Malamutes* by Father Bernard Rosecrans Hubbard, the "Glacier Priest." This priest drove his huskies eighty-five miles in sixty-seven hours. He camped out, crossed uncrossed glaciers, and climbed unclimbed mountains. Yet he never missed celebrating Mass or reading the daily prayers in his breviary! Ted wrote, "With him you will fight grizzly bears, fall into crevasses, starve, and yet come out unscathed—more fun than a barrel of monkeys."

In April of his senior year, Ted memorized massive amounts of the New Testament, so he could be Jesus in a play, *Mysteries of the Mass.* He worked on his lines as he walked to and from school, at the breakfast table, and before he went to sleep at night.

There were two hundred students involved in the three performances, but the local newspaper singled out Ted. "Particularly commendable was the portrayal of Our Lord by Theodore Hesburgh." One of Ted's classmates said, "You would think he was Christ!" Another added, "He *was* the play."

After the play, his friends stopped teasing him; they were convinced Ted would make a fine priest. In the senior class predictions of what each graduate would be doing in ten years, classmates envisioned Ted Hesburgh as "pastor of St. Peter's Church in Split Rock."

After spending twelve years at Most Holy Rosary, Ted Hesburgh graduated on June 24, 1934, earning awards for excellence in English and religion. Because he graduated third in his class, Ted was chosen to give the Address of Welcome. He thanked the nuns who "taught us all that we know, and what you have taught us we know to be the truth. You have prepared us for life's conquest even as the knights of old were prepared to fare forth against the infidel."

He thanked the parents of the graduates for their support and then concluded, "Father Time has turned another page in the book of life, and we stand upon the threshold of the coming years while the bright future beckons. May it be a happy one—as happy as the years gone by."

As he sat down, Ted spotted his mother wiping her tear-streaked cheek. Neither she nor Ted's father had been able to go beyond high school. She knew once Ted left the family home, he would never again call Syracuse home.

During his high school years, Ted and Father Duffy had kept in touch regularly. Ted's parents never pushed him toward the priesthood, but once he decided to enter seminary, they were delighted.

Ted had another decision to make. Did he want to be a diocesan priest working in a particular place like the Syracuse area, or did he want to join a religious order like the Jesuits or Franciscans? The diocesan priests Ted knew always seemed to be begging for donations. Instead, he decided to join a religious order and take a vow of poverty, thus making sure the rest of his life would be free from the tribulations of money-raising. Ironically, much of his time as President of the University of Notre Dame was spent raising and spending billions of dollars.

Ted decided to join Father Duffy's Holy Cross Congregation (in Latin, *Congregatio a Sancta Cruce*, abbreviated C.S.C.), with the hope of being a missionary in a foreign country. Missionary work demanded hardship and self-sacrifice, and it would provide the adventure he craved. (O'Brien p. 19)

When the time came to choose a seminary, Father Duffy gave Ted two options: The Eastern Province had a brand new seminary at Stone Hill College in Massachusetts; the Western Province was based at Notre Dame in South Bend, Indiana. It took Ted about one third of a second to decide. What Catholic schoolboy in the country didn't dream of going to Notre Dame?

So Ted Hesburgh refused a scholarship to Niagara University in New York and made plans to enter the Holy Cross Order at Notre Dame. The night before he left for seminary, he kissed all thirty-six girls in his class goodbye.

Chapter Four

# Right Where God Wanted Me to Be

SEVENTEEN-YEAR-OLD TED looked from his father to his mother and then to his sister Mary. He tried to fix their faces in his mind so he wouldn't forget how they looked. It was September 1934, and they had driven six hundred miles in a borrowed car to bring Ted to seminary at Notre Dame, Indiana. Soon they would climb into the car and travel back to Syracuse—without him.

All four tried to be brave until finally Mary lost control. Tears streaming down her face, she said, "I'll write to you every week, Ted." Then they were all crying and hugging Ted, telling him how much they loved him and would miss him. Ted's father pulled his handkerchief from his pocket and offered it to Ted's mother, who covered her face and sobbed. Her husband patted her shoulder reassuringly, saying in a ragged voice, "He'll be all right, Anne Marie. I understand they feed seminarians very well here at Notre Dame."

Ted wiped his eyes. Hoping he could keep his voice from quavering, he followed his father's hint and joked, "Mom, I may gain so much weight you won't know me the next time you see me."

"You fat? Never!" protested his mother, dabbing at her eyes. Ted's father clapped him on the shoulder. "Well, I guess we'd better be going," he said, turning to the car. Mary kissed Ted's cheek and jumped quickly into the back seat. His mother hugged Ted again. Looking into his eyes, she said, "Take good care of yourself, son. Dress warmly."

"I will, Mom. I promise."

Suddenly Ted was standing alone. With a lump in his throat, he watched the car get smaller and smaller until it disappeared around a curve.

Ted was immediately overwhelmed with homesickness. He wondered if he would be able to see Mary get her fine arts degree from Syracuse University. He had prayed for a brother practically all his life. Now he had to leave before nine-month-old Jimmy had even taken his first step! He didn't even have to close his eyes to see the home where he grew up, with its wide porch and white railing across the front of the house.

The previous day they had made the journey from Syracuse to Notre Dame. Mr. Hesburgh wasn't sure the family car could safely make the trip, so he borrowed one from a friend. As they were planning their route, they talked about taking a detour to spend a day at the World's Fair in Chicago. "A Century of Progress" was scheduled to conclude later that fall. Admission was only 50-cents, but Ted's father reluctantly decided they couldn't afford to go to the Fair. The country was still in the grip of the Depression.

They arrived at Notre Dame a day before Ted was due at the seminary, so they checked into a bed-and-breakfast. However, Ted had too much on his mind to sleep very well. The next morning they walked the seminary grounds on St. Joseph's Lake. Ted looked up at the giant oak trees and Gothic-style stone buildings. Things were so different from his bustling neighborhood in Syracuse! Ted felt like he had been transported back to the Middle Ages. He wondered if he would ever feel at home here.

Then they walked around St. Mary's Lake. Skirting its south side, they aimed for Notre Dame's main campus. They found a replica of the original log chapel built in 1831 by Father Stephen Badin, a missionary to Native Americans in the area. Nearby they spotted a Grotto like the one in Lourdes, France. Ted's father suggested, "Let's kneel down and say a Hail Mary for a good beginning to Ted's future."

Next Ted and his family headed toward the administration building with its famous Golden Dome topped by a statue of Our Lady (in French, *Notre Dame*).

"Take my hand, Mom," Ted invited. "Either we'll both make it up this steep hill or both slide back down." Ted's mother laughed—the ready laugh Ted loved so much.

They stopped in to pray at Sacred Heart Church, marveling at its Gothic spires, stained-glass windows, and golden high altar.

Ted's family accompanied him as he checked into Holy Cross Hall. College freshmen who intended to join the Holy Cross Order (known as postulants) stayed in this dorm on St. Mary's Lake. But now that his folks and Mary had left, Holy Cross Hall did not seem like such a great destination.

They were gone, and he didn't know when he would see them again. Ted opened the door to his room, sat on the edge of his bed, and stared at his trunk for a long time. He didn't have the heart to unpack just yet. That seemed too final. At last he lay down and fell into a fitful sleep.

A knock at the door woke Ted up. For a moment he couldn't figure out where he was. When he scrambled to answer the door, he saw Father Duffy standing there. "Hi, Ted," he said. "How about heading to the refectory with me for dinner?"

Ted had a hard time holding up his end of the conversation, so he was glad to listen as Father Duffy joked about his own first year in the seminary. However, when Ted got back to his room, he still felt overpoweringly homesick. He stared at his trunk again, but it would be almost a month before he finished unpacking. Instead, he pawed through the trunk each day and took out only what he needed.

Ted immersed himself in his classes and began to get to know the other postulants. He devoured letters from his sister Mary, who faithfully kept her promise to write every week. Every time he reread a new letter and put it aside, he found himself sighing. His homesickness seemed as endless as the long hours of study.

Ted spent most of his time at Holy Cross Hall, where all freshmen postulants took the same religion classes and socialized with each other. However, they did walk to the main campus for core classes with other university students. Ted kept up a lively banter with his fellow seminarians as they headed to Fr. Wenninger's life sciences class and Doc Hinton's chemistry class.

"What electives are you going to take next semester?" asked a classmate.

Ted wrinkled his forehead. "I can't possibly fit in everything I want to study," he confessed. "I want to keep up my Latin and study Greek, so I can read the New Testament. But there are three philosophy classes that sound fascinating too."

"I'm not even sure I know what philosophy is," said his friend.

"Oh, that's the study of what's ultimately real and true and how we know that," explained Ted. "I can see myself being a philosopher-priest someday."

"How about a literature class?" suggested his fellow postulant. "You're a pretty good writer."

"That's what I thought," admitted Ted, "until I got my final back from Father Leo Ward. He gave me a 95, but he wrote, 'If you don't learn to simplify your style..., you will wind up being a pompous ass.'" They both chuckled sheepishly. Father Ward demanded excellent writing of all his students.

During their first year, the postulants wore ordinary clothes like other college freshmen, but they lived under much stricter rules. As candidates for the priesthood, they could not date, attend coed parties, or write to girls they had known in high school. That was hard on most of the guys. Ted did miss his old friends, but they were scattered to different schools now, and he was focused on his own new life.

After a year, the seminarians began to wear special black clothes that made them even more of an enigma to other students. An article in the Notre Dame student magazine called them black-clad figures, shoulders hunched against the cold, which emerge from the northwest, attend classes, and then disappear. "Where the (seminarian) comes from and where he returns to is a mystery to many." (O'Brien p. 20)

The days before Christmas were especially bleak. Unlike other college freshmen, the postulants knew they would not be going home for the holidays. Ted felt very lonely and cold.

On Christmas Eve the postulants threw snowballs at one another as they walked over to midnight Mass. Then Ted said, "Race you to church." The snow made it tough going; no one had a clear lead. When they got close enough to see people converging on the church, one of them said, "We'd better slow down. After all, we're almost priests. We shouldn't be acting like high school kids."

Sacred Heart Church was beautifully decorated. Candles blazed everywhere, shedding their soft glow on a large crèche

set over to one side. Ted sang out the Latin responses heartily. After Mass the seminarians enjoyed a large, delicious
breakfast.

Late the next morning Ted sat down and wrote a long
letter to his family. He described the Christmas Mass at
Sacred Heart and promised to remember each of their inten-
tions as he said his rosary. He told them that even though he
loved and missed them all, he knew he was right where God
wanted him to be.

Chapter Five

# The Toughest Year
# I Ever Had

T ED'S FIRST YEAR OF STUDIES ENDED in the summer
of 1935, but he didn't return to classes. Instead, on
August 6, he hopped on a flatbed truck along with
twenty-nine other seminarians and twenty men who wanted
to be religious brothers. They were headed for Rolling Prairie,
a tiny town about thirty miles west of Notre Dame. There
they would spend the thirteen months of their novitiate on
a farm.

When they got off the truck, a brother and a priest met
them. After trading a few quips with the new arrivals, the
priest said, "Well, men, I'm Father Kerndt Healy, your Novice
Master and spiritual director. I'm here to help you listen to
God and say 'yes' to him, and to toughen you up spiritually."
Ted didn't think he looked very tough.

Then Father Healy said, "And this is Brother Seraphim."

Brother Seraphim spoke gruffly with a thick accent, "I
served in the German army during The Great War. My job
is to toughen you up physically. Father and I will test you
in different ways. I will train you in the discipline of the
priesthood through hard physical labor. That will weed out

those of you who don't have the will and stamina to be good priests. Much better you find out now, before it's too late."

With a sweep of his hand, Father Healy explained, "The Holy Cross Order bought this 720-acre farm last year. It's a little run-down, but we're going to make it productive. We hope it will provide enough food and firewood to fully support those of us who live here."

Brother Seraphim led them to the only new building on the place, where they would be sleeping and eating, praying and studying. Ted was impressed to learn that the previous year's novices had built this new house! It was big enough for each of them to have his own private room.

Before they reported to Brother Seraphim for farm duty, the novices went on an eight-day retreat. At the end of the retreat, they put on their special religious clothes for the first time, black robes called cassocks that came almost to the ground. Ted loved this prayerful beginning to his novitiate year. He felt anchored in the Spirit. Soon, however, Ted began to learn that there was more to becoming a priest than praying and studying.

Before long the novices began to call Rolling Prairie "boot camp" for the Holy Cross Order. Ted and his classmates rose at 5 a.m., but it was two hours until breakfast. First they spent half an hour in meditation, attended Mass, gave thanks to God, and then listened to a spiritual reading. After breakfast they cleaned their rooms and the corridors. Ted's chore was to wash dishes by hand. Because he disliked this task, he did it as fast as he could. He and two other guys got so they could finish washing the dishes and silverware for sixty people before the others even left the room. By 9 a.m. they were ready for a full day of farm work—unless a special task like harvesting crops or building a barn forced them to get up even earlier to start work.

Ted almost swallowed his tongue when Father Healy

announced that the novices must keep silence twenty-two hours a day, whether they were studying, praying, eating, or working. During meals, the novices developed their own sign language to request seconds. They held up four fingers for bread, closed a fist to signify potatoes, and pretended to milk a cow to have the milk pitcher passed down the long table. How Ted looked forward to the only two hours when they were allowed to converse: an hour after lunch and an hour after dinner each day!

After the novices built a barn, Ted knew how to drive a nail accurately and quickly. He felt great satisfaction the day they raised the sides and put on the barn roof. Near the barn they poured a circular cement foundation eighteen feet in diameter and two feet deep. Ted wasn't sure what it was for.

After getting up at 4 a.m. the following morning, they were trucked to an old silo, which stood fifty feet high.

The novices took turns standing inside the silo on a shaky circular scaffold that was raised and lowered with ropes. When it was Ted's turn, he stood on the scaffold and pried out one block at a time, using ropes and pulleys to lower it to the ground. Since each block weighed about fifty-five pounds, Ted's muscles ached as he helped load them onto a truck.

They climbed into the truck on top of the blocks and rode a short distance. When Ted saw the new barn and the circular foundation they had poured the previous day, he knew they were going to reassemble the silo block by block on that foundation.

In the middle of the afternoon, they sat down for a well-deserved rest, sure the day's work was done. Then Brother Seraphim declared in his thick German accent, "Now ve paint it."

His friend Tom nudged Ted and whispered, "What he means is, 'Now you fellows paint it.'"

"How do we do this?" Ted asked.

Brother Seraphim said, "You start at the top with a rope."

Still bewildered, Ted repeated, "You start at the top with a rope? I've never done this before."

"You will learn," Brother Seraphim promised.

He directed Ted to pick up a thick paintbrush and sit on a board suspended between two ropes. Then Brother Seraphim manipulated the ropes from inside, hoisting Ted to the top on the outside of the new silo. Ted didn't dare look down at the ground fifty feet below. Instead, he tried to concentrate on the paint job. A bucket full of whitewash hung on one side of his wobbly swing, a bucket of water on the other. Ted dipped his brush in the water then in the whitewash and painted the blocks with broad strokes. Somehow Brother Seraphim managed to pull him around the silo. Ted worked his way down level by level until both he and the silo were covered with whitewash.

Finally the job was finished. Ted opened and closed his cramped hands as he slid off the swing. All he could think of was getting into the shower.

That evening after dinner, Father Healy commented with a smile, "You looked very dashing up there today."

In late summer, the novices were again awakened at 4 a.m., this time to harvest the wheat and rye. They worked alongside all the neighbors from sunup till sundown. By noon, Ted was famished. He noticed long boards had been set on sawhorses in a neighbor's yard. Soon the farmers' wives processed out with platters piled high with steaks, mashed potatoes, corn and carrots. They set large foaming pitchers of milk on the tables. Ted helped himself to a steak as big as a tennis racquet and surrounded it with mounds of fresh vegetables. After tucking away all that, he still had room for a large piece of apple pie à la mode. That gave him enough energy to go back to work in the fields until it was almost dark. By that time, they had filled several thousand 200-pound sacks with grain.

One morning Brother Seraphim told Ted to gather honey from the beehives. Ted gulped. He had seen Brother come back from the hives covered with stings and welts.

Mentally rehearsing Brother Seraphim's instructions, Ted climbed the hill behind the barn. There the hives stood behind a barbed-wire fence to keep animals away. Ted looked back over his shoulder. He could see the small lake about fifty yards away.

Ted crawled under the barbed wire. As soon as he took off the tarp covering the hive, bees swarmed into his hair and ears, down his neck, and up his pants. He grabbed the rack of honey, set it down, replaced the tarp, shoved the case under the barbed wire, and scrambled under the fence, carefully avoiding the barbed wire. On the other side, he picked up the rack and streaked down the hill, running as fast as he ever had in his life. Still covered with bees, he burst into the barn and practically threw the rack at Brother Seraphim.

Then Ted raced to the lake and dove in. After staying under water several seconds, he stuck his nose out. The bees seemed to have given up, so he waded out and fell down on the grass to catch his breath.

There was no end to Brother Seraphim's ingenious work details. The novices dug a sewer line under a road and cleared fields of rocks, weeds, and sumac bushes. They felled trees, with Tom McDonagh on one side of a two-man cross-cut saw and Ted on the other. Then they sawed the logs into three-foot lengths. Finally they split the logs into firewood to heat the central building. Agh! Ted felt pain above his knee. He had come too close to the cross-cut saw. He carried the scar the rest of his life, a permanent reminder of his novitiate year at Rolling Prairie.

One day a thunderstorm sent the work crew running for the barn. All smiles, they were sure they would get at least a short respite from their backbreaking work. But Brother Seraphim couldn't let his charges sit idle. He announced, "I want each of you to get a sheep, bring it back and pick the lice off it." Ted quickly learned how to squeeze each louse to death between the nails of his thumb and forefinger. Two hours later, when all fifty sheep had been deloused, Ted stank—and he was full of lice! That night he bathed in Lysol.

In November, Ted helped butcher a pig. The four novices' first task was to catch the pig. Then each hung onto one of the animal's legs for dear life while Brother Marinus clunked it over the head with the broad side of an ax and slit its jugular vein. Meanwhile, another novice held out a pan to catch the blood.

Next the carcass was dunked in a vat of boiling water three times to make its hair come off.

"How can you tell when it's ready to come off?" Ted asked.

"That's easy," explained Brother Marinus, who grew up on a farm. "You just pull on the pig's tail. If it comes off, the rest of the hair will come off too. Like this." With that, he pulled the tail off so fast he lost his grip and it flew straight into Ted's face. Yuk! The rancid smell was so strong Ted had to grit his teeth to keep his breakfast down. Then they scraped off the rest of the pig's hair.

After slicing around the pig's neck, they grabbed both ears to twist its head off. Then they hung the carcass on a hook and split its whole front side open. Ted plunged his hand into the gore and pulled out the heart, liver, and kidneys.

Ted sloshed several buckets of hot water into the abdominal cavity. That reduced the stench somewhat. Then they spread-eagled the pig front down on a board and used a knife to split it along the spine. Ted and Tom McDonagh each lugged a half to a storage cooler at the house.

Next day they cut the pig into hams, bacon, and ribs, then melted its fat for lard. Nothing went to waste. Leftover parts like ears, nose, and lips were ground up and mixed with herbs to make sausage.

Fifty years later, Father Ted could still describe the butchering process in vivid detail: the squeals, the stench, the feel of plunging his hands into the gore. Amazingly, he never lost his taste for pork.

During the winter, there was less to do in the fields, so the novices studied and attended lectures in addition to their household and farm chores. Throughout the day they had set times for the Liturgy of the Hours, the common prayer of the Catholic Church.

Despite this rigorous schedule, Ted managed to read over one hundred books during his year at Rolling Prairie. Most were on spiritual topics, but Ted combed through the library for books he might find more interesting than the very old, dry ones that were read to them every day.

When Holy Week came, Ted was chosen to do a reading from *The Imitation of Christ* by Thomas à Kempis during the three-hour Good Friday service. Before the service, he still had to do his farm job, shoveling manure away from the little pig houses where it had been stacked up all winter to keep the pigs warm. He had to run upstairs and take a quick shower so he wouldn't smell like a pigsty in church. He hadn't been able to finish his work, so after the service he took off his cassock and returned to spreading manure.

In the spring it was time to plant corn, wheat, and rye. They knelt down and placed four kernels of corn into each mound of earth. Neighbors helped them plant their acreage, and the novices helped their neighbors. Ted watched the sweet corn poke through the earth and begin to grow higher and higher. How he hated to thin the corn by pulling out the weaker shoots. Then a drought set in, and the crop withered. They had to grind up one hundred acres worth of corn for chicken feed. None of it was fit for the table.

One day Father Healy stopped Ted and asked, "Would you take a picture of me in this new cape I received from Rome?" Ted obligingly took the picture, and then the priest said, "As long as you're here, I might as well take a picture of you." Only after he snapped the picture did he say, "Oh, I forgot, you novices aren't supposed to have your pictures taken. Can't have you getting too vain."

A month later, Ted received a letter from his mother. She told him how nice it was of Father Healy to send her the picture of Ted dressed in his cassock. Ted smiled to himself. Perhaps Father Healy felt a little sorry for him. The other novices' parents came to visit occasionally, but Ted's parents lived too far away.

Toward the end of Ted's time at Rolling Prairie, a new class of novices arrived to begin their "boot camp." Father Healy told him, "I'd like you to give a one-hour lecture every day to the incoming class." All Ted said was, "I'd be honored," but he couldn't believe his good fortune. After keeping silent twenty-two hours a day for a year, he would get to talk to these guys an extra hour every day!

Ted took his own inventory at the end of the thirteen months. They had started with twenty-nine novices, and only nine were left. The other twenty slipped away one by one without even saying goodbye. One day a person wouldn't show up for a meal. Then the others knew he had left.

Ted said to Tom, "It's been a tough year, but I'll bet those of us who have made it this far are going to be priests for life!"

"We're not quitters," Tom agreed.

When Ted left Rolling Prairie, he was pleased to be in the best physical shape of his life. He weighed 145 pounds, without an ounce of fat on him. And he knew one thing for sure: he never wanted to be a farmer.

On August 16, 1936, Ted made his temporary vows of poverty, chastity, and obedience, promises he would have an opportunity to renew after three years. He moved into Moreau Seminary. After Rolling Prairie, Moreau seemed cozy and homelike—except for the bells. There were bells to start and end class, bells to announce choir practice, work details, study periods, and recreation periods. He grew to hate those bells!

Along with their prayer, study, and singing, the seminarians had their "grunt work." Ted's job was waiting tables for priests, seminarians, and laymen on retreat. Again he pulled the job he hated most: washing dishes. Ted's four-man crew washed dishes for about a hundred diners. Again they got the technique down so well that only minutes after a bell signaled the end of the meal, they had finished washing and drying the dishes and put them back on the shelf.

Toward the second year of taking college classes, Ted wondered if the people in charge thought he had what it takes to make a good priest. Unbeknownst to him, his professors and religious superiors had noticed what a good student he was. They were about to send him in a new direction that took him completely by surprise.

Chapter Six

# Last American Ship
# Out of Rome

T ED WIPED THE SWEAT OFF HIS FACE. It was July 1937, and his room on the top floor of the seminary was sweltering. Only one more exam and his sophomore year would be over. Before taking a final look at his class notes, he loosened the fastening on his heavy cassock. He knew a seminarian was supposed to keep it on all the time, but he was sorely tempted to strip down to shorts.

As if his superior knew he was contemplating this small disobedience, Ted heard a sharp rap at his door.

"The boss wants to see you," announced a classmate. Trembling a little, Ted hurried to the assistant provincial's office, cassock flapping as he turned the corner. With an expressionless face, Father Ted Mehling looked up from his desk and handed Ted a piece of paper. Ted was pretty sure it must contain his obedience, or next assignment, but why the special summons? Wasn't he going to be studying at Notre Dame again next year with all his classmates?

As if he had voiced his question, the priest said, "This is for you. You're going to Rome to study next year."

"I am?" gulped Ted. He glanced down at the familiar

form. As always, it began with the words: "The obedient man shall speak of victory." Written below that was: "Theodore Hesburgh has been assigned next year to study in Rome." It was signed by Father Burns, the provincial of the Holy Cross Order.

Father Mehling added, "Oh, McDonagh is going too. Would you send him in for his paper?" Too stunned to ask any questions, Ted backed out of the office and went looking for his friend Tom.

After Tom got his obedience, the two of them thought of a dozen questions. When would they be going and for how long? How would they get there? Where would they stay? What would they need to bring? Why had they been chosen? Most important of all, why were they going to Rome at all? What would they be doing there?

After supper, they mustered their courage and went back to Father Mehling. Their questions tumbled out, but they got no answers. Father Mehling said, "School in Rome doesn't start until November. You'll be spending the rest of this summer at the order's summer camp in Lawton, Michigan. That's all you need to know for now."

As they left the office, Tom turned to Ted in confusion. "How can he say that's it? There are a hundred things I need to know!"

Ted agreed. "I haven't seen my family in two years. I sure hope we get to go home before crossing the ocean!"

Finally the two seminarians were able to make an appointment to see Father Burns. "Let's take a walk," he suggested.

So they paced back and forth behind the administration building and Sacred Heart Church, plying Father Burns with questions. Father Burns specialized in terse answers, but by persistent questioning, they managed to learn a few details.

They were to embark September 25 on the *SS Champlain*, a French ship. Yes, they would get to spend two weeks at home with their families before that. The order would pay for travel from their homes to New York City, but they had to pay their own way home. Ted grumbled to himself and wondered how he could afford that. Tom lived only eighty miles away in East Chicago, but Ted had to get all the way to Syracuse.

Finally they got Father Burns to answer the question that had been burning in their minds: What would they be doing in Rome?

"Oh," he answered casually. "You're each going to get a doctorate in philosophy and a doctorate in theology."

Ted wasn't sure he'd heard right. "Two Ph.D.s?" he asked.

"Sure," Father Burns replied. "You'll be able to do it. You're going to be there for eight years."

Ted's mouth fell open. Eight years? That was nearly half as long as he'd been alive. By the time he came back to the States and saw his parents again, he'd be twenty-eight!

Just before Ted and Tom left Notre Dame, their superior figured how much money they would need for travel expenses. For Ted, Father Burns calculated bus fare from Syracuse to New York City, the cost of cheap hotels in New York and Paris, a five-dollar tip for the ship's steward, and rail fare from Paris to Rome. Coming up with a total of nineteen dollars, he wrote a check, folded it, and handed it to the young seminarian.

Ted swallowed hard. He couldn't help thinking Father Burns must be the chintziest guy God ever created! However, Ted managed to mumble a polite thank you. Not until they had left the office did he unfold the check. Then he discovered it was written for one hundred dollars, plenty to cover their travel expenses, including the fare from Notre

Dame to Syracuse. The two young men could hear Father Burns chuckling behind them.

So Ted headed home for two weeks. He couldn't believe how much Jimmy had grown up since his last visit. The preschooler could actually carry on a conversation as well as roughhouse with his big brother. The time in Syracuse flew by. Before he knew it, Ted was on a train bound for New York City.

During his layover there, Ted visited his Grandfather Hesburgh for what turned out to be the last time. By this time the old man was completely blind from macular degeneration, which would later affect his grandson as well. Ted walked into his grandfather's one-room apartment at 9 p.m. He could hear the radio playing, but he couldn't see a thing.

"Where's the light switch?" he asked.

"How should I know?" Grandfather answered. "What good is a light switch if you're blind?" So Ted groped for a chair, and the two of them sat in the dark. Memories about his grandfather tumbled together in Ted's mind. He remembered hearing Grandfather say the same phrase in seven different languages—and now Ted was headed to a foreign country where he could learn new languages firsthand! He also recalled how the tragedy of losing his wife and two tiny sons had alienated Grandfather from the Church.

Knowing his grandfather hadn't gone to church in a long time, Ted pleaded with him. "Here I am giving my whole life to God, and you don't even believe in him!"

Grandfather Theodore shot back, "I didn't say I didn't believe in him." This response puzzled Ted. They began arguing intensely, neither willing to back down.

Finally Ted blurted out, "The only way I'm going to get you back to God is to pray and sacrifice a lot for you."

"You do that," replied Grandfather.

When he got to Rome, Ted kept his promise by saying extra rosaries and many prayers for his grandfather. When he skipped dessert or a cigarette he really wanted, he asked the Lord to please accept this small sacrifice as a way of praying for his grandfather to turn his heart to God and go back to the Church.

Not long afterward, Ted's cousin wrote that their grandfather had asked her to take him to the local parish. He celebrated the sacrament of penance and resumed going to Mass. When he died peacefully in a Catholic hospital a few months later, the news made Ted's grieving heart soar.

As their train pulled into Rome, Tom and Ted stretched and rubbed their sore necks. They had been sitting upright for twenty-four hours since leaving Paris, and they were exhausted. But they strained to catch a glimpse of the Eternal City.

"I think I could easily sleep this whole day away," yawned Tom.

"I'm tired, too," admitted Ted, "but there's so much to see! Do you suppose they'll let us do a little sightseeing before we buckle down to work?"

"At least St. Peter's and Vatican Square!" agreed Tom. "After all, it is the heart of the Catholic Church!"

"But I'm starving!" exclaimed Ted.

Sure enough, once they arrived at the three-story house on the Via dei Cappuccini, a meal was the first order of business. And what a meal! Omelets, Italian flat beans, Bel Paese cheese, and *sfilatini* (little loaves of Italian bread).

During and after the meal, they were lectured by Père ("Father" in French) Sauvage, the superior of the seminary. Père Sauvage had a strong opinion about everything. He said, "Smoking, that's not good for anyone. But drinking, that's another thing entirely. Over the next several years you will drink a good deal of wine while you are in this house.

But you will never get drunk, I promise you! You will learn to drink rationally."

When he discovered they'd traveled second-class on the train from Paris to Rome, he was scandalized. "What a waste of money! Why do you need to sit on cushions? After this you crowd into third class and sit on hard wooden benches, with the poor."

It was 10:30 p.m. before Père Sauvage finished his harangue. Since no classes were scheduled for the next day, the young men hoped they would be allowed to sleep in. No such luck.

"You will all rise at 5 a.m. tomorrow," declared Père Sauvage.

When some of the seminarians groaned, he continued, "We rise at 5 a.m. every day, work or no work, school or no school. There are no holidays here."

Their schedule was simple but demanding. Every day began with prayer, Mass, and a breakfast of bread, cheese, and coffee. The tiny hot-water heater meant each resident could take only one hot bath a week, and there was always a line to use the bathroom. It reminded Ted of sharing a bathroom at home with his three sisters. He tried not to dwell on that memory, though. It made him homesick.

At least he had a bowl and a pitcher of water in his room, so he could shave and wash up there—if he could break the ice in the pitcher! The marble floors in the house were so cold in the winter it was like walking on snow barefoot. During January, Ted's fingers were too numb to type class notes in his room.

After breakfast, Ted and his fellow students spent fifteen minutes walking to classes at the Gregorian University. At noon, they came back to the residence for chapel and lunch before returning to classes.

They arrived back at the Collegio di Santa Croce (Holy Cross College) at 3 p.m. every afternoon. "Form two lines at the front door," directed Père Sauvage.

Ted grinned at the seminarian standing opposite him. "Looks like we're partners today," he said. "How's your Italian? Shall we try chatting with any of the merchants?"

Père Sauvage made sure each seminarian was clad in his thin cassock and a round black Roman hat with a broad brim. On colder days, they added a *douillette* (a long black coat). Then they set off at a brisk pace. Besides giving him exercise, these jaunts introduced Ted to every corner of Rome. How he loved turning a corner and coming upon a marble statue, a splashing fountain, a ruin from Roman times, or an imposing church façade. Often they had to move aside for goose-stepping Italian soldiers going through maneuvers in public squares. When that happened, they quickly changed direction.

After their walk, there was time to study before chapel and a light supper. Ted used the half-hour allotted for recreation to interact with his housemates by playing cards or ping pong.

Around 9 p.m., Ted went to his room to sleep or to study. He was allowed to stay up as late as he liked, as long as he arose at 5 a.m. the next morning.

Ted's childhood interest in "what was over the next hill" came to the fore as he met students at the Gregorian from almost every country in the world. But they all put aside their native languages when they entered the university. Classes were taught and exams were taken entirely in Latin.

"You mean we even have to learn Hebrew in Latin?" he asked incredulously. But soon he was able to speak fluent Latin, even take notes and type them up in Latin.

Since Père Sauvage was French, only French was spoken in their residence, including chitchat. When they were out on the streets for the daily afternoon walk, they spoke Italian. Ted also set about learning Spanish from a Mexican classmate. Between his Spanish and Ted's Italian, they were able to understand each other well enough to become good friends.

"Languages seem to come so easily to you," said an admiring classmate. "How do you do it?"

"I promised myself once I got to Rome, I'd never speak English if I could help it," Ted explained. "I do love languages, but it's not automatic. Before lunch every day, I spend fifteen minutes learning thirty new words: ten in Italian, ten in French, and ten in German. I review the thirty I learned yesterday, and take a peek at the ones I plan to learn tomorrow. We're learning Hebrew and Greek to read Scripture, and I hope someday I can learn Russian, Japanese, Chinese, and Portuguese too."

"But why?" his friend persisted.

"I like to communicate with people," Ted answered. "I want to understand different cultures, and you get that best by hearing and speaking their own language."

"I feel so silly when I try to say something in Italian," his classmate admitted. "How do you do it?"

"I don't know. I just barge in," said Ted.

Ted wasn't sure how to answer the question his sister Mary asked in an early letter. "You asked what it's like studying at the Gregorian. Well, I don't think teaching methods have changed here since it opened in 1558! I'm so glad I get to read original works, the best ever written in these subjects, but I have to admit they make my head ache sometimes."

It was hard to tell how well he was doing. There was only one exam in each course, at the end of a whole year of study. At least the seminarians knew exactly what they had to master. The content of each course was summarized in fifteen true statements. Besides memorizing those statements, they had to be prepared to think on their feet, presenting arguments proving any of the fifteen summary sentences the professor happened to choose.

"I'm ready for a break," admitted Ted toward the end of his first year in Rome. "I can hardly wait for our vacation at the House for Spoiled Priests in the Tyrol."

"Vacation?" questioned Tom. "Even though we don't have classes at the Gregorian for two months, we're not going to be lying around in the sun or hiking the Alps. Père Sauvage expects us to keep learning all summer."

"But we can set our own pace!" exclaimed Ted. "And we get to sleep in till 6 a.m., with scheduled common prayer only twice a day. That will make me feel like the priests who used to be sent here for a break and some therapy."

After Tom heard what Ted hoped to study over the summer, he whistled. "Don't you ever ease up?" he asked.

Ted gave him a puzzled look. "If I go through a day and don't learn something, I feel like I've wasted the whole day," he explained.

Père Sauvage reluctantly approved Ted's ambitious program. He wasn't sure Ted could do it all, but by the end of the summer Ted had worked through a German language textbook. Not only was he able to chat with local villagers, but he had read the whole New Testament in German as well.

Ted also read two long philosophy books, one in French and one in Italian. For lighter reading, he chose *The Betrothed*, a novel in Italian, and a history of Italian art, since he knew the seminarians would stop in Florence to see the art of Michelangelo and other masters on their way back to Rome.

By being in the right place at the right time, Ted witnessed an important moment in Church history—the election of a new Pope. After Pope Pius XI died in February 1939, classes at the Gregorian were suspended for several weeks until all the Cardinals could gather and elect the next Pope. With everyone else in Rome, Ted and his classmates eagerly watched the smokestack at the Vatican. A black puff of smoke meant the Cardinals had conducted a round of balloting and failed to agree on a new Pontiff.

Father Ted would remember for the rest of his life where he was standing in St. Peter's Square when a white puff of smoke signaled the election of a new leader for the entire Catholic Church.

"Any guesses who it is?" queried a classmate.

Before Ted could answer, the dean of the College of Cardinals appeared on the balcony above the square. His words reminded Ted of the angel's message to the shepherds in the fields outside Bethlehem. "*Annuntio vobis gaudium magnum, habemus Papam...*" ("I announce great joy to you, we have a Pope...") The crowd held its collective breath until the dean finished his sentence, "the most reverend and most eminent Eugenio... who has chosen for himself the name of his predecessor." In that moment, Cardinal Eugenio Pacelli was first presented to the faithful as Pope Pius XII.

"I know him!" exclaimed Ted. "Last year Cardinal Pacelli spoke at Notre Dame. I don't remember his talk. I just remember all my classes were canceled for the day. Guess I should have paid more attention to what he said. But who knew he was about to become Pope?"

In an article that appeared in Notre Dame's *Ave Maria Magazine* in August of 1940, Ted described the reaction of the crowd in St. Peter's Square when the new Pope came out. "On all sides, people knelt and blessed themselves as his voice, strong and firm, pierced the dusk and gripped us with an indescribable feeling of trust and confidence... All about the city, jubilant church bells were ringing, adding to the already exuberant spirit of the hour...We hurried past historic monuments, careless, and for the moment almost heedless of their age-old significance. Tonight we had been living history—the glorious history of a force that outlasts even these ancient piles of Imperial days." (O'Brien p. 27)

Although the seminarians were focused on Church matters and their studies, they couldn't ignore the fact that Europe was headed toward war. Benito Mussolini had been the sole dictator of Italy for fifteen years, building up that nation's military power. In 1935, Italy had conquered Ethiopia, and the next year Mussolini formed an alliance with Hitler's Nazi Germany. By the time Ted and his classmates arrived in Rome, this "Rome-Berlin Axis" had added another strong partner, a war-like Japan.

"Gentlemen," Père Sauvage told them shortly after they arrived, "you are here to study theology, not to be involved in politics. However, you should be aware that Mussolini's official quarters are right behind the Gregorian. Unfortunately, this may disrupt your studies at times."

Ted soon found out what he meant. Every time German despot Adolf Hitler came to town, classes at the Gregorian were called off for a week.

"Why should we have to miss classes just for that?" Ted asked an older seminarian.

"Have you taken a look at the roof of the Gregorian?" his housemate answered. "It would be pretty easy for a sniper to climb up there and train his weapon on the Führer."

"Hey, Ted, come over to the window," classmate Bill

Shriner called excitedly one day during their enforced break. "You'll be able to see Hitler passing by."

Ted knew Hitler was touring Rome in an open car, but he also knew all about the dictator's brutality to "inferior races" like Jews, gypsies, and anyone who disagreed with him. He shot back, "I wouldn't walk ten feet to see that bum!"

In speeches that made Germans cheer, Hitler declared that Germany needed "*lebensraum*" ("room to live"). In March 1938, he declared Austria a part of Germany. Czechoslovakia was next, in October. Italy quietly took over Albania in April, 1939.

"Why don't the British and French do something?" Ted wondered aloud.

Bill shrugged. "Hitler keeps saying this is it; he won't attack anyone else. They want desperately to believe him. Nobody wants another war so soon after the last one."

"What about our own country?" Ted asked. "Surely we could do something to stop the Nazis!"

"Have you seen an American newspaper lately?" Bill asked. "Americans seem to think this European war has nothing to do with us."

American tourists flocked to Europe during the summer of 1939, but France and Great Britain realized that Hitler's next target was likely to be Poland, since a section of that country lay between two portions of Germany. They signed an agreement to defend Poland if necessary.

The axe fell on September 1, 1939, when Hitler invaded Poland. France and England declared war, but they were too far away to stop the German "*blitzkrieg*" ("lightning strike"). Soon Poland, too, was in Nazi hands.

Yet Ted's studies continued uninterrupted. "Are we in any danger here?" he asked Père Sauvage. "What does your government think?"

"I don't know," admitted the French priest. "My country is placing its confidence in the Maginot Line, the fortifications it's built in the mountains between us and Germany, but I have my doubts. We'd better pray hard."

Toward the end of Ted's third year of studies, the American consul came into his 10 a.m. class to announce that the Germans had invaded Belgium and the Netherlands, making an end run around the Maginot Line and marching toward a shocked France.

"Are any of you Americans?" the consul asked. "You've got to be out of the country in a week. The last American ship, the *USS Manhattan*, leaves Genoa next Friday. If you're not on it, you probably won't be able to get out of Rome until the war is over, and no one can predict how long that will take or how much fighting there may be in this city itself."

The announcement stunned the seminarians. Instead of five more years, their studies in Rome would come to an end in a week. They had only days to prepare for final exams and gather all their belongings.

Ted panicked. He had kept up in all his other classes, but he had counted on being able to cram for his Hebrew language exam during that final month. Instead, he would have to take an oral exam on the whole year's Hebrew studies before June 1—with all the questions and answers spoken in Latin.

After staying up to study for twenty-four hours, Ted faced his professor. He was able to answer the first three grammar questions: "He kills," "She kills," and "He will kill," in Hebrew, but "He was killed" stumped him. He had to answer "*Nescio*" ("I don't know") to that one.

He knew his next task would be to translate a Scripture passage from Hebrew into Latin. His heart pounded, since he'd only read as far as Genesis. A Hebrew Bible was lying on the desk in front of Father Galdos.

"*Legas*," he told Ted in Latin ("Read"). He spun the Bible around so Ted could see it.

Ted couldn't believe his eyes. The Bible lay open to the first few verses of Genesis. Not only had Ted read it in Hebrew, he also had memorized the Latin version of those verses, so he had no trouble translating from Hebrew into Latin! The examiner gave him a six—the lowest passing grade—but pass he did.

On his way out, the professor said, "*Buen viaje*! ("Have a good trip!) Send me a postcard from New York, please."

While the Americans were embarking from Genoa in June of 1940, three hundred thousand French, Belgian, and British soldiers got into any boat they could find and fled from Dunkirk, France, to England. Hitler and his allies were now in control of all of Europe except Switzerland, which managed to remain neutral.

Ted's trip across the Atlantic took ten days. The ship had to take evasive measures to avoid German submarines.

When the boat docked, Ted was already at the rail. He spotted his sister Mary on the pier, waving to get his attention. He charged down the gangplank and hugged her.

"I was afraid with this terrible war that I might never see you again," she admitted. "But you look wonderful."

Ted hugged her again. "I'm glad to be back," he smiled. "How's Mom? How's Jimmy? How's everyone?"

"Come on," Mary urged, "We don't need to do all our catching up here on the pier!"

"I'm so glad they're giving me two weeks at home!" Ted grinned. "When's the next train for Syracuse?"

"It leaves in about two hours. We can make it if you don't have any other business in the city."

"Just one small thing. I promised to send Father Galdos a postcard."

Arm-in-arm, they headed away from the harbor, lugging Ted's trunk behind them.

After two wonderful weeks at home catching up with family and friends and eating the best of his mother's cooking, Ted had to leave. Again he had no idea when he would see his family again.

Instead of Rome, Ted finished his graduate studies in Washington, D.C. He was an excellent student, completing his doctorate in two years instead of three, yet he was very aware of World War II unfolding in Europe and Asia.

On December 7, 1941, the Japanese bombing of American ships anchored in Pearl Harbor, Hawaii, brought the United States into the war. Sixteen million young Americans joined the Army, Navy, and Marines. A patriotic American, Ted asked his superior to assign him to a Navy aircraft carrier in the Pacific as chaplain.

All he got back was his next obedience: to finish his studies at Holy Cross College then move on to Catholic University for his doctorate.

In the middle of those studies, Ted's lifelong dream came true.

Chapter Seven

# What I Always Wanted to Be

T ED STOOD AT THE BACK OF Sacred Heart Church
waiting for what seemed like an eternity. But after
wanting to be a priest for twenty years, what did a
few minutes matter?

The date was June 24, 1943. Ted and fifteen other young
men were about to be ordained. With so many people
crowded around him, Ted could feel his white alb sticking to
his back. He wiped the sweat off his forehead and turned his
heart to the Lord. He made a prayerful promise to celebrate
Mass at least once a day every day for the rest of his life.
The Catholic Church didn't require this, but he felt it was
the least he could do to thank God for the incredible gift of
being a priest.

Finally Ted heard the first solemn notes of the organ.
Slowly, slowly the line began to move. A great number of
Holy Cross priests had come for this special day. Behind
them, Ted could easily spot Bishop John F. Noll because
of the pointed miter on his head. He carried a crook that
showed his job was to shepherd the people in his diocese,
which included the University of Notre Dame. At last it was

time for Ted and the other candidates to process down the aisle. He carried the heavy priestly robe over his left arm.

On his way down the aisle, Ted tried to locate his family. There they were, right up front! Before he passed their pew, Ted could hear ten-year-old Jimmy's stage whisper. "Here comes Ted!" Out of the corner of his eye, Ted saw Mary elbow Jimmy and hold her finger to her lips.

As Ted approached the altar, Bishop Noll made the sign of the cross and then said in Latin, "I will go unto the altar of God."

Ted responded heartily, "To God who gives joy to my youth."

He took his place and continued the prayers until he heard the archdeacon say, "Let those who are about to be ordained to the priesthood come forward."

With heart-felt confidence, Ted replied, "I am here." As he knelt, he heard the archdeacon declare that he, Theodore Martin Hesburgh, was ready to be ordained.

After a long prayer, he lay face down on the cold marble floor, showing his submissiveness with his body.

As he lay on the floor, Ted could feel his heart beating rapidly. He could hear the choir singing a long litany of the saints. "Holy Mary, pray for us...All ye holy Angels and Archangels, pray for us."

Finally the pivotal moment came. Ted got up from the floor, shaking with excitement. He knelt down. When it was his turn, he felt Bishop Noll lay both hands on his head, making him a priest forever. All his brother priests of Holy Cross filed by, each one in turn laying his hands on Ted's head in silent prayer.

One rich symbol after another unfolded. The Bishop rearranged Father Ted's stole the way only a priest can wear it. Then he took the chasuble, the heavy robe Ted had been carrying all this time, and put it over Father Ted's head. "Receive the priestly vestment, by which charity is signified," said the Bishop.

"Thanks be to God," responded Father Ted.

When it was his turn, he knelt in front of the Bishop again, holding out both hands. The Bishop dipped his thumb in sacred oil and anointed the new priest's hands. Father Ted stared down at those hands, feeling the oil and smelling its perfume. Filled with awe, he realized these very hands would hold the host as it became the Body of Christ.

After the ordination, the Mass resumed. But this time, Father Theodore M. Hesburgh, C.S.C., said the prayers along with the Bishop. He spoke them loud and clear.

After Communion, Father Ted knelt before the bishop once more. This time Bishop Noll gave him the power to forgive sins. Then he covered both of Father Ted's hands with his own and asked, "Do you promise your Bishop reverence and obedience?"

"I promise," declared Father Ted. He knew his promise included not only Bishop Noll, but also Father Ted's Holy Cross superior, Pope Pius XII, and all the men who would hold these positions in the future.

Then Bishop Noll kissed his right cheek and said, "The peace of the Lord be always with you."

The Bishop concluded the two-hour Mass with a pep talk. Then he invited the new priests to join him in giving the congregation the final blessing. As they processed back down the main aisle, Father Hesburgh joyfully sang the final hymn of praise.

Father Ted was eager to connect with his family, but well-wishers reached out to offer their congratulations. Suddenly he felt his little brother tackle him from the side. Father Ted grasped Jimmy's hand and followed him through the crowd.

Soon his overjoyed mother was reaching up to hug him tight. Tears welled in her eyes as she whispered: "Now you are Father Ted!"

His dad clapped him on the shoulder. "Son, is this a good time to give us your first official blessing?" Father Ted stretched out his hand and made the sign of the cross over his mother and father, his brother, and each of his three sisters.

Together they headed for the door on the east side of the church. After Father Ted passed through it, he turned back and looked at the helmet engraved above the doorway.

Jim followed his gaze. "What are all those names?" he wanted to know.

Father Ted read the words aloud: " 'Our Gallant Dead.' Jim, those are the Notre Dame graduates who gave their lives in World War I. When I see it, I can't help thinking about all the young men who are dying every day in this Second World War."

Under the helmet, Father Ted read four more words: "God, Country, Notre Dame." He lingered a moment to dedicate his own life to the love of God; the love of country; and the love of Notre Dame, Our Lady and her university.

Then he noticed Jimmy looking up at his white collar.

"That shows I'm a priest." Father Ted leaned over and hugged his ten-year-old brother. "I'm going to wear it from now on. If people need help, and they see that Roman collar, they'll come to me. So Jim, if you or your friends ever need help, I'm your man."

Jimmy broke the solemnity of the moment. "I'm starving," he said. "Isn't there a party where we can get something to eat?"

"Sure," smiled Father Ted, "Back at the seminary." As they walked down the hill, Jimmy stuck to him like gum on a shoe. On the path between the two lakes, Betty said, "I remember that you made promises of poverty, chastity, and obedience for the rest of your life, but I really don't understand what that means for your everyday life."

"Those promises free me to do whatever God wants," Ted explained.

"But why would you want to be poor?" Anne chimed in. "I sure don't."

"A vow of poverty frees me to use material goods to serve others, not myself," Father Ted explained. "I'm confident God and the Holy Cross Order will always make sure I have everything I need, as long as I don't get greedy."

Father Ted linked arms with Anne. "Haven't you noticed how people get trapped by money? Either they don't have it, and they're always trying to get it, or they have it, and they have to worry about keeping it or getting more. I'm free from all that!"

"Haven't you ever wished you could get married and have kids?" Betty asked.

Father Ted smiled. He knew his sister was sweet on a soldier. "I don't think I could ever love a single human being the way I love God.

"Since I don't belong to one special person," he continued, "I belong to everyone. Each time someone calls me Father, I want to give him the compassion and understanding he needs."

"Hey, Ted—I mean Father Ted," Jimmy interrupted. "All this talking is slowing us down. There won't be any chocolate cake left!"

Father Ted punched his brother playfully and quickened the pace.

"But what about obedience, Ted?" Mary asked gently. "That's got to be the hardest vow of all."

"You're right," admitted Father Ted. "I've already had to

do a lot of things I'd never choose to do, from butchering a pig to going to Rome. Sometimes my superiors ask me what I want to do and sometimes they don't, but you know what? Every time I've swallowed hard and obeyed, it has turned out much better than what I would have chosen for myself."

At the reception Father Ted introduced his family to the other priests, and then found them a table. As they ate, Mary asked, "What comes next, Father Ted? You've studied in D.C. for three years. Now will you be assigned to a parish church like most new priests?"

"You know the desire of my heart," Father Ted declared. "Now that I'm a priest, I'm itching to serve as chaplain aboard a Navy aircraft carrier in the Pacific. We've been involved in World War II for two years, and I'm tired of being on the sidelines. I want to be part of the action."

"And what does your superior have to say about that?" asked his father.

"He wants me to finish my graduate studies in Washington first."

"Well, I'm just happy you'll be coming home for a bit before you go," said his mother, putting her hand over his. "Everyone at Most Holy Rosary is eager for your first Mass, Father Ted." She couldn't help smiling when she used her son's new title.

After Father Ted's first Mass in Syracuse, he headed back to Washington, D.C., and plunged into his studies at Catholic University. But because so many priests were serving as chaplains with the fighting men overseas, requests for his help began to pour in. These requests took time away from Father Ted's schoolwork, but he was glad to help out.

"Can you hear confessions at St. Martin's?" Father Bill asked. "At least until you get your regular parish assignment?" Father Ted worked at St. Martin's for two weeks. He found the pastor there a great role model. Whenever they got into the parish car, the backseat held something for the needy—baby clothes for an unwed mother, a birthday cake for an eighty-year-old parishioner. As he rode along, they chatted.

"I understand you're working on a doctorate in sacred theology," said Father Bill. "How much longer will that take?"

"Ordinarily three more years," said Father Ted, "but if I push myself, I think I can finish at Catholic U. in two."

"Really?" Father Bill whistled. "That sounds like quite a workload!"

"The second year will be a killer," admitted Father Ted. "I'll have to take six courses, with a long paper due in each, and be writing my dissertation at the same time."

"And does a dissertation still mean writing five hundred pages on one topic, with ninety pages of footnotes listing books you've read in six languages?"

"Yup," said Father Ted. "You can see why delivering a birthday cake is a nice break for me."

Later that week, Father Ted met with his dissertation adviser, Paulist Father Gene Burke.

"Any ideas for your thesis topic?" asked Father Gene.

"I want to write about Catholic Action," said Father Ted. "I first heard about it when I was in Europe. I know most people feel like bishops and priests should be in charge of everything in the Church and tell everyone else what to do, but that's not right. Baptism gives every Catholic the ability and duty to bring God's love into the world."

"I couldn't agree with you more," said Father Gene. "But you'll never get that topic approved at this university. It's much too practical."

"Hmm," replied Father Ted. "What if I gave it a longer

title? How about *The Relation of the Sacramental Characters of Baptism and Confirmation to the Lay Apostolate?*"

Father Gene chuckled. "That just might work," he agreed.

And it passed!

Soon Father Ted was assigned to St. Patrick's. The priest he replaced gave him some practical advice: "When you answer the doorbell, spend time with the person at the door. Don't be satisfied until you know why that person rang the bell."

The first time a beggar came to the door, Father Ted loaned the man five dollars. The other priests in the rectory laughed at him. "You'll never see that money again," they predicted.

Father Ted defended himself. "I'd rather get tricked ninety-nine times out of a hundred than miss helping the one person who really needs my help."

A week later, the man sent Father Ted an envelope containing five dollars. He enjoyed waving it around the rectory.

One sweltering day, Father Ted was wading through a book on Catholic Action written in German when his telephone rang. "Father Patrick O'Toole here. Can you give a three-day retreat for a thousand high school students?" he asked. "The priest who was scheduled had to cancel."

Father Ted pleaded with him, "Look, I've only been ordained two months, and I have nothing with me that would help in giving the retreat."

"Oh, you can do it," he replied.

And Father Ted did. He gave three talks a day, counseled the boys, and heard their confessions.

Soon he found himself helping out as a chaplain at Fort Myer and in the federal reform school as well.

Father O'Toole had another request: "Would you lead a three-hour Good Friday service?"

"What time does it start?" Father Hesburgh asked.

"At noon."

"That's only half an hour from now!"

He heard a familiar response. "Oh, you can do it." And he did.

"Would you help run the USO club while I'm on vacation?" Father Dade asked. "It's not such a good part of town, but our service men and women really need a place to relax. We've hired military bands, so all you have to do is be on hand in case there's trouble or anyone needs a listening ear."

So Father Ted watched fifteen hundred soldiers and sailors jitterbug all night.

Father Ted met thousands of young servicewomen at the USO. They came to him for guidance and for confession, but he wished he had some written advice to hand them. The National Council of Catholic Servicemen jumped at his offer to write such a pamphlet.

He wrote a letter to his sister Betty, who was in the WAVES (Women Accepted for Volunteer Emergency Service), a division of the Navy. "There are a lot of Catholic Women in the WAVES, and I want to write pamphlets for them. I'd like to begin each one, 'Dear Betty.' Thinking about you while I write will help make it more personal."

Father Ted prayed that the Mother of God would inspire women in the service "to give our darkened world a shining example of Christian womanhood." His advice in the booklet was down-to-earth: Be cordial and kind to the other women…Simple tasks like writing a letter and answering the telephone "are worth eternity if done for Him and with Him." (O'Brien p. 31)

After the pamphlets were issued, Father Ted was perplexed. They had printed as many copies as there were women in the armed services, but it kept selling out. Who was reading them? Then one night he walked into the USO club and noticed a male sailor reading one of the pamphlets. As soon as he saw the priest, the sailor quickly tucked it into his pocket. Father Ted realized he had to write inspirational booklets for men too.

Of course Father Hesburgh's main writing project was his dissertation on Catholic Action. For two years he had been reading books and articles on the topic. Now he had to pull it all together.

By 5 p.m. on March 1, 1945, he was supposed to turn in five copies, typed with no errors. Because computers and copy machines hadn't yet been invented, this required hours and hours of careful typing—with two fingers!

When he shared his plight, Jim Norris, director of the National Council of Catholic Servicemen, said, "Father Ted, for the past two years you've written so many booklets for us and never expected any payment. Tell you what I'm going to do. I'm assigning my five best secretaries to type up your dissertation."

On March 1, Father Ted paced nervously up and down the room where the secretaries were hard at work. Would they be done by the 5 p.m. deadline? The sound of pounding typewriter keys filled the room. A bell rang every time a typist reached the end of a line. Then she had to pull the carriage return lever to get down to the next line.

The fastest typist finished her manuscript and handed Father Ted the pages. Carefully he used a pen to put in accent marks, added each page to the stack, and made sure all the edges were perfectly lined up. Then he slid the pages into a manila envelope.

Finally the fifth secretary pulled the 500th page out of her typewriter and handed it to Father Ted. He looked anxiously at his watch. 4:50 p.m. It would take him nearly half an hour to travel across town to the theology department office at Catholic University where he had to turn in the dissertation.

With trembling fingers, he dialed the department secretary's number. "It's done!" he told Helen O'Connor.

"Thank God!" she exclaimed. "Don't tell Monsignor Fenton, but I'm going to keep the office open until you get here. But you'd better hurry!"

Phew. Father Ted didn't even realize he'd been holding his breath through the whole conversation. Now all he had to do to earn his S.T.D. (Doctor of Sacred Theology) was to meet with a group of readers and convince them what he had written was correct. He received the degree on May 23, 1945.

Father Ted's cousin, a Navy captain, arranged for him to be a chaplain on an aircraft carrier. All he needed was his religious superior's permission. He wrote to Father Tom Steiner:

"I would still like very much to do a priest's work with the boys who will have a man-sized job on their hands in the Pacific." However, Father Ted knew that "the decision is entirely in your hands."

He sent off his request on May 6 and waited anxiously for an answer. A week, then two weeks went by.

Finally the letter from Father Steiner arrived. Father Ted tore it open. It said he could go home to visit his family for a week. But on July 5, 1945, he was to report to Notre Dame to begin teaching. Father Steiner explained that thousands of officer candidates would be coming to Notre Dame to study. There weren't nearly enough professors to teach them all.

Disappointed, Father Ted finished packing and headed home. A month later the war in the Pacific ended. Father Ted was about to become chaplain for all the returning veterans at Notre Dame. He felt as if the Lord said, "Your planning is terrible. Leave it up to Me."

### Chapter Eight

# Chaplain Anyway

"YOU MEAN THERE ARE NO course outlines for dogma and moral theology?" Father Hesburgh exclaimed in disbelief. It was Friday, and he had just arrived back at Notre Dame with his Ph.D. "How can I start teaching Monday morning?"

"I'm afraid that's right," replied Father Simonitsch, the new head of the religion department. "Every priest who teaches one of these courses has a different approach."

"That doesn't seem fair to the students," said Father Ted. "Everyone has to take four religion classes, but from the title, he can't tell what they're about."

"Exactly. That's why I'd like every course with the same title taught the same way," the chairman agreed. "How about making outlines for the dogma course as you go? You know Father Charles Sheedy from grad school, right? I've already asked him to write notes for moral theology. See what you two can come up with!" he said, walking Father Ted toward the door.

"Who's teaching other sections of my course?" asked Father Ted. "Think I'll start by seeing what they're doing."

Looking over the list of teachers, he whistled. One was a chemist, another had studied American history. Father Ted was the only one who had earned a graduate degree in theology. Since all were priests, they knew the content of the dogma course: what the Catholic Church believed and taught. But he was sure they would appreciate some direction in how to present it.

Father Ted walked into Father Charlie's office and shook his friend's hand. "Sounds like you and I have an extra assignment," he said.

"Yup. It'll be great working together again," Father Sheedy replied. "But this sounds like more of a challenge than the booklets and newsletters we pounded out in D.C."

"Guess I'd better get to work," said Father Ted. "I'll try to have my outline for the first dogma class done in time for you to look it over before we give it to the other teachers. And I'd appreciate seeing your plan for the first moral theology class as well. You're not going to use that antiquated textbook they gave us, are you?"

"Not on your life," said Father Sheedy. "Good grief! Students need to know more about right and wrong than how late they can come into church and how early they can leave and still have it count as fulfilling their Sunday obligation to go to Mass!"

"So you've been at this for a while, Charlie. Any tips for a greenhorn?" Father Ted asked.

"Where are you bunking?" his friend wanted to know.

"I'm the rector in Badin Hall," Father Ted replied. "I know that involves saying daily Mass, counseling, and taking care of the students who also live there. What else can you tell me about that dorm?"

"I think many of the residents are veterans. They're not

straight out of high school. Some of them have been in enemy prison camps, and they've seen their buddies killed."

"Hmm," mused Father Ted. "That might call for a special approach."

"Well, you always did want to be a chaplain. Here's your chance!" Father Sheedy said.

Father Ted thought for a moment. "These men are over twenty-one, old enough to have a beer now and then. I know Notre Dame has very strict rules about not allowing alcohol on campus, but what if I let them keep a beer in the refrigerator in my room?"

"They'll be your friends for life," Father Sheedy promised.

The two men brainstormed for hours about the content of their courses. Then each worked to put the material into a form other teachers could easily use. Often Father Ted was up long after midnight typing notes for the class he had to teach the next day.

\* \* \*

About a year after he returned to Notre Dame, Father Ted got another taste of a chaplain's life. The adventure began one day when he answered a phone call from Father John Cavanaugh, Notre Dame's president.

"Ted, the Secretary of the Navy has asked me to join an ROTC cruise. It'll be out in the Pacific for six weeks, and I just don't have time for it. Would you mind doing it for me?"

"Father John, that's like offering a steak to a hungry dog," he replied.

Before long, Father Ted found himself eagerly boarding the *USS Princeton,* an aircraft carrier bound for Hawaii. As they cruised, he watched planes take off and land. His old desire to fly kicked in, stronger than ever. Finally he got to take a ride in a torpedo bomber. What a great flight!

Once in Hawaii, Admiral John McCrea asked, "Father Hesburgh, how about leading us in a short grace before lunch?"

"Of course, I'd be glad to," replied Father Ted, "but I don't want to step on anyone's toes. Shouldn't one of your official Navy chaplains do it?"

"I have no stomach for that," said the Admiral. "It takes too long, and I'm hungry. Those chaplains all feel obliged to tell the all-knowing God everything that is going on."

Father Ted stood up and made the sign of the cross. Then he led the standard Catholic grace before meals: "Bless us, O Lord, and these thy gifts, which we are about to receive from thy bounty, through Christ Our Lord, Amen."

The admiral patted Father Ted on the back. "I'd like to do you a favor for that short grace. Is there anything you'd like to do while you're here?"

"I love to fly. Any chance I could go up in a plane?"

"I think I can arrange that. Where would you like to go?"

"I'd love to see the big island, the one that gives Hawaii its name."

"Great. I'll arrange for you to fly in the Tearjerker squadron."

"The what?" asked Father Ted.

Admiral McCrea smiled. "We dubbed it 'Tearjerker' because the planes get so wet flying through storms to collect weather data."

"That's more than I could have hoped for," said Father Ted gratefully. "I'll say a short grace for you any time you like." Both men chuckled.

Two days later, Father Ted boarded the lead plane along

with a reporter from the *Chicago Daily News*. Eager to try out a new camera, the reporter asked if they could fly to the island of Maui so he could film the crater of Haleakala Volcano.

Shortly after takeoff, Commander Davis asked Father Ted, "Have you ever piloted a plane?"

"No," answered Father Ted, "but I'd love to learn how."

"Done," said Davis. "Come on up here and trade places with my copilot."

Father Ted concentrated on each instrument as the pilot showed him what it did and how to make sure it was working properly.

"Haleakala Volcano, coming right up," announced Davis.

"Think I'll try to get some photos from the Plexiglas bombardier station," the newsman said, moving down to the nosecone.

Before Father Ted knew it, the plane dove into the crater at 150 miles an hour. It zigzagged across the bottom, narrowly missing six-hundred-foot high cones.

Suddenly Father Ted saw a thousand-foot high wall looming ahead! His heart stood still. Clearing his throat, he said, "Sir, you do see that cone just to our left, don't you?" At the last possible minute, Davis turned and sped back to the other side.

For a moment Father Ted wondered if they would spend the rest of their lives flying back and forth in that crater. Then Davis headed straight for a V-shaped opening. Father Ted could see that it was narrower than the plane's wingspan.

"This is it, the end," he murmured to himself. He didn't even have time to pray. To his amazement, the pilot stood the plane on its wing, perpendicular to the ground, and whizzed through the V.

Davis asked, "How about it, Father? Would you like to go into the crater again?"

"No, sir!" he shot back.

Father Hesburgh's adventures weren't over. On automatic pilot, the plane headed for a second volcano, Mauna Loa. The plane slid over the volcano, clearing it by a whisker.

After landing on the Big Island (Hawaii), they toured a fern forest, volcanic tunnels, and an inn atop another volcano, Kilauea. Then it was time to fly back to Hickam Air Force Base.

A little way into that flight, Commander Davis said, "Padre, you've had a flying lesson. Now, by golly, you're gonna fly!" With that, he left the cabin and lay down for a nap.

Flying the plane was more complicated than Father Ted expected. The plane swayed back and forth and bobbed up and down. One wing dropped, pulling him off course. He straightened the wings parallel to the horizon in front of him. A picture of an airplane on the instrument panel showed him they were climbing. He eased the plane down to the right altitude. He had to stay constantly alert, making adjustments to fit whatever conditions he encountered. He felt like he was driving a big, stubborn truck on a narrow, winding road.

Without explanation, the copilot left his seat. Even though Father Ted had plenty to do, he felt pretty lonely in that pilot's seat. He flew solo for about twenty nerve-wracking minutes before the pilot woke up and came forward to land the plane at Hickam. After all, he hadn't taught Father Hesburgh anything about landing.

\* \* \*

After this excursion, Father Ted returned to Notre Dame and resumed teaching his six courses, turning his outlines into a textbook, and taking care of the students in Badin Hall. At the beginning of each year he memorized the name of each student in his dorm.

One night a vet asked, "Father Ted, we're planning a party this weekend. Could we store a keg of beer in your apartment?"

"Nothing doing," Father Ted answered. "One beer is fine, but the first time I took a group of vets on a beach outing, I learned my lesson. Once a keg is opened, students feel like it has to be used up, no matter how drunk they already are. I'm not going to be responsible for anything like that again!"

Many of the students who came to Notre Dame after the war were married, and they soon began to have children. Before long, Father Hesburgh was faced with a new problem.

"I plan to marry my sweetheart over Christmas break," one of the students from Badin told him. "But I can't find a place to live off campus. I've looked at half a dozen apartments. If they're decent, we can't afford them. Those we can afford are filthy and falling apart. What am I going to do?"

"Can you do me a favor, Joe?" Father Ted requested. "Keep looking and answering ads. You and your bride should rent the first decent place you find. When you're ready to move out at the end of your studies, we'll get another couple to sublet it from you. On your hunt, please make me a list of places other Notre Dame students can live safely and inexpensively."

"I'll be glad to do it," Joe answered, "but you know students aren't allowed to have cars. I could do the job much faster if you could get me permission to drive around and look."

"I'll see what I can do," promised Father Ted. But the problem of housing for married students nagged at him. He wondered what the Army was doing with all the barracks they weren't using any more.

Soon he was able to bring some of those temporary

buildings to Notre Dame to create housing for over one hundred families in what became known as "Vetville." And Father Ted became their chaplain.

One morning Father Hesburgh was walking across campus when he met a young Vetville wife. "Good morning, Betty. How are things?"

"Okay, I guess, Father," she said, wiping away a stray tear and trying to smile, "but I sure wish I lived closer to my mom. I'm kind of worried because I wake up every morning feeling so sick to my stomach."

"Betty," he told her with a big smile, "I think you should make an appointment with a doctor. Sounds to me like you might be pregnant." As she walked away, Father Ted shook his head. As an unmarried priest, he never expected to be giving that kind of advice.

Soon he had another problem on his heart. Many Vetville wives were losing their babies shortly after they found out they were pregnant. He began looking through his prayer books until he found a blessing for pregnant women.

"Betty, can you help me get the word out?" he asked. "Anyone who's pregnant or even thinks she might be pregnant can come to my apartment at one p.m. on the first Monday of every month for a special blessing."

They came, and the early miscarriages stopped just like that. Father Hesburgh kept careful track. He rejoiced when he counted thirty-nine normal deliveries in a row without a single miscarriage. But he also grieved with Bill and Helen O'Connor when they lost their first baby during the sixth month of Helen's pregnancy.

Six months into Helen's second pregnancy, Bill called Father Ted in the middle of the night.

"I hate to bother you, Father, but can you come down to the hospital? Helen's in labor again."

"I'll be right there," Father Ted replied.

As he sat in the waiting room at three a.m. with Bill, a nurse came out and told them, "It's a boy. He only weighs 3½ pounds. Do you want to come in and see him?"

"How is he?" Bill wanted to know.

"His heart's beating," the nurse answered, "but we're having trouble getting him to start breathing."

With the staff's permission, Father Ted immediately baptized Mark with a cup of very cold water. The baby gulped in a mouthful of air and let out a lively howl.

"Your son was born into time and eternity at the same time," Father Ted told Bill.

Passing a water fountain on his way back to the operating room, Father Ted leaned over to take a drink. In those days, the Church did not permit a Catholic to receive Communion if he had eaten or drunk anything, even water, after midnight. Father Hesburgh realized right away that his thoughtless swallow of water meant he would not be able to say Mass that day. It was the first and last time he broke his promise to say Mass every day, but he wouldn't have missed being there to baptize that baby for anything in the world.

Besides saying Mass for the couples in Vetville, baptizing their babies, helping them with their studies, and giving advice on everything including money, Father Ted tried to arrange inexpensive recreation. He was able to get another building the Army didn't need any more. There he sponsored dances featuring student musicians. Students paid a quarter to get in, which included a pop. When fashions changed and women's skirts got longer, Father Ted insisted the women wear the old styles—because he knew few of them could afford to buy new clothes.

Vetville became a very close community. When a nine-month-old baby died from spinal meningitis, Father

Hesburgh went door-to-door holding a milk bottle. By the time he finished his rounds, the bottle held enough money to send the couple to Connecticut, where they held their daughter's funeral.

One night at two a.m., Father Hesburgh got a phone call. The young husband on the other end of the line sounded desperate. "Sorry to bother you so late," he said, "but we're in the middle of a terrible fight. I can't get her to stop crying!"

Father Ted sighed. "I'll be right over," he promised. As he buttoned his shirt, he prayed, "Come, Holy Spirit."

An hour later, he felt peaceful going back to his room. Without taking sides, he had helped these young spouses listen to each other and work things out.

Experiences like this helped Father Ted realize Notre Dame needed a good course on marriage and family life. So he developed one. Students flocked to take it.

So all day Father Ted taught religion courses, and at night he often babysat in Vetville, charging the young parents only a beer and a sandwich.

* * *

After three years as chaplain to the veterans in Badin Hall and Vetville, Father Hesburgh was given a new assignment: head of the religion department and rector of Farley Hall. There he was in charge of 330 freshmen straight out of high school. They had a whole different set of problems. Some needed to learn how to study. Some had no idea how to make their beds or separate clean and dirty laundry. Away from home for the first time, they sometimes had trouble settling down after lights-out. It was usually midnight by the time Father Ted was free of responsibilities for his students and could begin banging away on his typewriter, trying to turn his course outline into a religion textbook.

Father Hesburgh and Father Sheedy each wrote a textbook that was used in Catholic colleges for many years. Father Hesburgh's book, *God and the World of Man*, sold over 100,000 copies after its 1950 publication.

Father Hesburgh loved teaching at Notre Dame and relating to the students, workers, and other teachers. He would have been happy doing this until he retired, but God had other plans for him.

Chapter Nine

# A World-Class Catholic University

O NE DAY IN JUNE 1949, Father Ted sat in the cool basement chapel of Sacred Heart Church. As the youngest priest there, he knew he would be the last one to receive his "obedience" for the coming school year. And he was pretty sure he knew what it would be. He loved teaching and being a chaplain. Sure, Father Cavanaugh, President of Notre Dame, had asked if he would like to help run things, but Father Ted had given him a firm "no." Sitting behind a desk wasn't for him.

As he listened to other priests' assignments, Father Ted realized that the president had done some restructuring. There were now vice presidents in charge of several different areas.

Then Father Mehling announced, "Ted Hesburgh, Executive Vice President."

Father Ted was stunned.

On the way out of the church, he buttonholed the president. "Father John, what is an executive vice president?"

"Oh, that's the vice president in charge of the other vice presidents," Father Cavanaugh answered.

Father Ted groaned. The other vice presidents were all older and far more experienced than he. How could he tell them what to do?

Father John had high expectations. "Ted, I'm really going to load it on you, and you're going to hate me, but best you learn in a hurry," he said.

"I could never hate you," Father Ted replied. But he couldn't help wondering where all this was headed.

One of the first things the president taught his new executive vice president was how to make decisions. "Don't ask: 'What is the easy thing to do?' Don't ask: 'What will cost the least money?' Don't ask: 'What will make me the most popular?' Simply ask: 'What is the right decision?'" (O'Brien p. 52)

One of Father Ted's first assignments was to write strict new rules for the athletic department, then go to every game and make sure they were being followed.

"You want me to do what?" he asked Father Cavanaugh.

"Choose an athletic director who will report to you and tell Coach Leahy what to do."

"Father John," Father Hesburgh objected, "Frank Leahy has been doing as he pleases as long as he's been here—with great results. Of course I'll do whatever you want, but I need to know one thing."

"What's that?" asked Father Cavanaugh.

"When Coach Leahy hits the ceiling and refuses to do it my way, are you going to back him or me?"

"You."

"Even if you lose your football coach?" asked Father Ted.

"Well, we can survive that," Father John concluded.

Father Ted drew up the new rules and sent them to Coach Leahy: No more free tickets from anyone but the president of Notre Dame. The team doctor, rather than the coach, would decide when an injured player could get back on the field. No more than thirty-eight players could travel to an away game, as Big Ten rules specified. As executive vice president, Father Ted was to approve the list of players and get them excused from their classes.

Before the first away game in the fall of 1949, Father Ted learned that there were forty-four players on the list. When he threatened to expel the extra six, Coach Leahy caved in and pared down the roster, but he fumed all through the long train ride to Seattle.

During the game against the University of Washington, the referees were clearly unfair in their calls against Notre Dame. The Fighting Irish managed to win the game anyway, but the press gave Coach Leahy a lot of flak for criticizing the referees. Father Hesburgh defended the team and their coach. This helped the two men make peace with one another.

Before Father Ted went to a game, Father John would call him into his office and say, "Oh, I've got some friends I want you to meet at a luncheon. Treat them well." Many of these people soon made donations to Notre Dame.

During another meeting Father Cavanaugh assigned Father Ted to oversee and inspect new construction.

"But, Father John," he objected, "I know nothing about construction. I know nothing about architects or contractors. I know nothing about materials or finances. You want me to be in charge of building five new buildings?"

"You'll learn," smiled Father Cavanaugh.

Father Ted swallowed hard. "I guess I'll have to."

Because he had never done this before, he questioned the way things had always been done. Why didn't Notre Dame get bids from more than one firm? Why not start with how a building would be used instead of how it should look?

He wound up saving Notre Dame $84,000 on one project alone.

Notre Dame's finances were pretty shaky, but Father Ted never gave up. In one memo he wrote, "The only silver lining in the above dark cloud is the Lady on the Dome who has brought us [this] far without a budget. Maybe we should begin the budget meetings with a prayer to the Holy Spirit and end them with a Hail Mary." (O'Brien p. 51)

The only way Father Ted could handle so many different responsibilities was to focus his full attention on one job at a time. When it was done, he moved on to the next without wondering whether he had made the best decision. He stopped worrying, said his prayers, and went to sleep.

But one day in January, Father Ted's responsibilities suddenly increased. Standing in Father Cavanaugh's office, Father Ted noticed that the older man looked very pale.

"I hate to do this to you, Ted," he said, "but I feel terrible. They don't know what's wrong with me, but my doctor wants me to go down to Florida and get some sun. I'd like you to take care of things for six to eight weeks."

Father John filled Father Ted in on everything that was happening at the university. Then he smiled, picked up a huge pile of mail, and dumped the letters into Father Ted's lap. "You can get started by answering these letters," he said.

Father Ted turned thirty-five on May 25, 1952. A month later, he once more found himself sitting in Sacred Heart's basement chapel awaiting his "obedience." But this time there were no surprises. For three years Father Cavanaugh had been getting Father Hesburgh ready to take over.

Earlier that week, the provincial called him into his office and said, "You're about to be named president of Notre Dame. Which men should I assign as vice presidents to support you?"

"I'll have to give that some thought, Father Mehling," replied Father Ted. "But I'm sure of one thing: I want Ned Joyce as my executive vice president. He's a great guy, and he's good at everything that doesn't come naturally to me, especially handling money."

As he sat in the chapel and listened to the list of vice presidents, Father Hesburgh nodded at each name. There was a brief pause then he heard, "Ted Hesburgh, president." His stomach flipped nervously.

On their way out of church, Father Cavanaugh handed him the key to the president's office.

That was it. There was no retirement party for Father John and no formal ceremony to install Father Hesburgh as president. "Just get right to work," Father Cavanaugh said. "Good luck. I'm off to New York."

"Oh, by the way," he said, "I promised to give a talk tonight to the Christian Family Movement. Now that you're the president, you have to do it."

Father Ted turned the key in the lock and opened the door to his new office. He whistled. Father John had cleared off the desk, but his books were still on the shelf. Father Ted walked over to the bookcase and ran his hand across their spines. It was comforting to have some tangible reminders of the man who had taught him how to be a leader.

He looked out the window, remembering Father Cavanaugh's words: "Leadership is simple. All you need is a vision of where you want to go and the ability to inspire a lot of people to help you get there."

He sat down behind the desk to get a feel for his new role. It wasn't hard stating his vision. He wanted Notre Dame to be the greatest Catholic university in the world. Simple, but not easy! He knew the university had a long way to go.

The door was still ajar, but he heard a firm knock. He

looked up and smiled warmly when he saw Father Ned Joyce, his executive vice president.

"Well, President Hesburgh, how does it feel?" he asked.

"A little overwhelming," Father Ted admitted. "At least I know I'll only have this job for six years. Then I can go back to teaching."

"So where do we start?" asked Father Ned.

Father Hesburgh ticked off his priorities. "A great university needs a great faculty, a great student body, great facilities..."

"Well," said Father Joyce, "Notre Dame does have one thing going for it. It isn't just a lot of separate parts operating around a central heating plant. It's already got a great spirit."

"Amen," agreed Father Ted. "Come, Holy Spirit."

"A great student body," repeated Father Ned. "What are our goals for our students?"

Father Ted tapped his pen thoughtfully on the desk. "First of all, we want our students to be good men. Then we want them to be good at what they choose to do in life. Finally, we want them to make a positive difference in the world."

Father Ned smiled and nodded. "A great faculty," he continued. "If we have good teachers, we'll attract strong students."

"That may be tricky," admitted Father Ted. "In some departments, things have been done the same way for years and years. If we're going to improve, I'm going to have to fire teachers who aren't doing a good job."

"It would be easier if you didn't care so much about people, wouldn't it?"

"Yes," agreed Father Hesburgh. "I plan to delegate as many decisions as I can, but I have to take final responsibility for firing, hiring, and promoting teachers. I know I'm dealing with people's lives. If the answer comes out no, the man or woman is finished here in another year. If it comes out yes and he's thirty-five years old, we'll have him for the next thirty-five years. That's huge." (O'Brien p. 264f.)

"Great facilities," continued Father Ned.

"If we attract all the students I'm hoping for, we'll need more buildings. That means I'll have to raise money—lots of it." Father Ted rubbed his forehead. "Well, Ned, it's a comfort to know you're in the next office when I yell, 'Help!'"

Father Ted tried to inspire Notre Dame's professors. He told them, "Students react positively to a great vision of what they and their world might become...in truth, justice, beauty, the good and, yes, in love, too. If we are unclear or less than enthusiastic about this, who will follow the uncertain trumpet? Certainly not our students." (O'Brien p. 256)

There was one more "great" Father Ted found impossible to ignore. Many people in the United States knew only one thing about Notre Dame: it had a great football team. He struggled to find the right role for sports in the university. When Father Ted held press conferences, reporters often asked about the football team's prospects. More than once he replied, "If that's all you want to talk about, this news conference is over. I'm not the football coach." (O'Brien p. 56)

After one such press conference, Father Joyce confronted his boss. "Be careful, Ted," he warned. "If people think you're de-emphasizing sports, donations to the university are going to dry up."

"Well, Ned, you know how I feel," Father Ted retorted, "We don't apologize for football. Notre Dame wants to be best in everything. We want the best professors and the best coaches, in the right balance. I'm very glad when our Fighting Irish win games, but the heartening thing for me is that this university is beginning to become known for other things besides football." (O'Brien p. 56)

However, Father Ted did enjoy rooting for Notre Dame.

Ara Parseghian, head football coach from 1964 to 1974, tells this story. "We were going to play Alabama in the Sugar Bowl. Both of us were undefeated and the national championship was on the line. We were at this dinner and Father Hesburgh walked over and he kind of nudged me. He said, 'You know I've never asked you for anything in these ten years, but it would please me very much if you could win tomorrow.'" (Hunnicutt p. 30)

The Irish won by one point.

Five years later, in the 1979 Cotton Bowl, Quarterback Joe Montana led Notre Dame to a 35–34 comeback victory over Houston. After the game, Father Ted got down on the field and led the band as it played the Victory March. Surprised, a referee teasingly questioned this "overemphasis" on football.

Father Ted replied, "There's a time and place for everything, and that was the time and place for that." (O'Brien p. 291)

As his six-year term as president of Notre Dame drew to an end, Father Hesburgh felt like he'd been running a hundred-yard dash for six years. He felt ready to be done with it, but two things became clear to him and his superior: He was very good at what he was doing, and he had launched the university on many new projects that remained unfinished.

Like all Notre Dame presidents before him, Father Ted had been the religious superior of the Holy Cross priests at Notre Dame. In order to have enough time to do a good job as president, a different priest became superior. That made it possible for him to stay on as president—for twenty-nine more years!

One afternoon, Father Hesburgh and Father Joyce were chatting. "Did you see the game on TV last night?" asked Father Ned.

"Ned, you know I don't have the time or inclination

to watch TV," Father Ted answered. Just then there was a knock on the door. Father Ted recognized John Schneider and invited him in.

"Father Hesburgh," John began, "Television has so many exciting possibilities for our students. What would you think of building a TV station on campus?"

"That would give our journalism students a big edge," said Father Ted. "Tell me more."

"You think it's a good idea then?" asked John.

"Run with it. Just keep me informed."

One day Father Ted asked himself a radical question. Priests of the Holy Cross Order had always made decisions for the university as its board of fellows. But didn't that limit Notre Dame's growth toward greatness? He mused about bringing in experts in business, law and other professions, even if they weren't priests. The more he thought about this idea, the better he liked it.

This was a big change, and many priests opposed it, but Father Ted found it surprisingly easy to get the world leadership of the Catholic Church to approve the change. In 1967 it took the Vatican two days, and the payment of a fee of 1500 lira (about three dollars), to approve transferring control of about half a billion dollars in assets from a board of priests to a board that included lay members.

The new board of fellows had six priests and six lay people. Since every decision had to be made by a two-thirds majority, neither group could overrule the other. There was also a group of over fifty talented trustees who advised the fellows.

Father Ted used his considerable powers of persuasion to get the very best people to serve as trustees. In 1985, the president of a large corporation turned down his invitation to chair the Board of Trustees. That is, he refused until Father Ted took him and his wife out to lunch in their hometown.

Father Hesburgh said, "One of these days, in the not-too-distant future, you will be confronting St. Peter at the gate. When you get there, he is going to say, 'What did you do?' If you say, 'Well, I did very well; I was the president of an international company,' he won't even know what you're talking about. If you say, 'Among other things, I served as Chairman of the Board of Trustees of the University of Notre Dame,' you'll walk right in."

Recounting this story, the man reported, "By the time we got to dessert, my wife and I looked at each other and we knew it was the right thing for me to do." (O'Brien p. 184)

As Father Ted was striding across campus one day, he looked up at the golden statue of a woman on top of the administration building. Then he looked at the students hurrying by on their way to classes. Not one of them was a woman!

As soon as he got back to his office, he broached the subject. "Ned, for its first 130 years, Notre Dame has admitted only men. And I've always taken that for granted. But what do you think about having women students here?"

"Whoa," said Father Joyce. "That's a huge change. You know how it is right now. If a girl—say, a student's sister—happens to walk on campus, windows go up and everyone stares at her till she's out of sight."

"I realize we'd have to do a lot to make it work," agreed Father Ted.

"And how would our alumni feel?" continued Father Ned.

"Well, it's been on my mind for a long time," said Father Ted. "I'm going to start trying to make it happen."

In the fall of 1972, Notre Dame quietly admitted 365 women. Now about half the students are female, "And I have to say it's a much better institution," says Father Ted.

Admitting women and having lay people on the governing board were major changes, and Father Hesburgh had many more accomplishments as president of the University of Notre Dame. By the time he retired in 1987 at age seventy, he had spent half his life in that position. But Father Ted gives God most of the credit, "There must be a special providence that watches over Notre Dame. Good things happen to the university, and no one really knows the reason why. But it's been like that since Father Sorin founded Notre Dame." (O'Brien p. 53)

During those thirty-five years as president, Father Ted had more of an impact beyond Notre Dame than he could ever have imagined. He profoundly influenced American higher education, the Church, race relations, international human development, and world peace. At Notre Dame, his personal concern touched the lives of individuals in all walks of life, including students, parents, teachers, and ordinary folks—whether they cleaned his office or repaired his car.

Father Ted in front of "Touchdown Jesus" mural on the Hesburgh Memorial Library

Anne Murphy Hesburgh with her three oldest children (l. to r.): Ted, Betty and Mary

Seminarians at Collegio di Santa Croce in Rome with their superior, Father Georges Sauvage (second row, right), Ted in middle of second row

Hesburgh family at Lake Ontario before Ted leaves for Rome, September, 1937;
Back row: Ted, Mary, Betty; Front row: Anne, Mrs. Hesburgh (Anne), Jimmy, Mr. Hesburgh (Theodore B.).

Father Ted dances with a Notre Dame female student at a picnic celebrating his 25th anniversary as President of the University; the first women were admitted in 1972.

Father Ted links arms with Martin Luther King, Jr., at a 1960 civil rights rally in Chicago.

Colonel Franklin D. Shelton, Commander at Beale Air Force Base, congratulates Father Ted after his flight in the F-71 at age 61.

"Hooked for life," Father Ted displays one that didn't get away.

Chapter Ten

# Any Student Could Climb Up and Knock on My Door

C HAUFFEUR MARTY OGREN stifled a yawn as he spotted Father Hesburgh striding down the hallway in Chicago's O'Hare Airport.

"Thank you, Marty, for coming to get me," said Father Ted. "I'm sorry it's so late. I was booked on an earlier flight; then I learned that one of our students had been in a terrible accident. I couldn't leave D.C. without going to the hospital to see him."

"Do they expect him to recover?" Marty asked.

"Yes, God willing, but it may be a long haul. I don't think he'll be able to finish the semester on time."

Father Ted climbed into the car.

"I brought your mail," Marty said.

"Thanks so much," said Father Ted, opening the attaché case. "Do you mind if I turn on the light?"

When they pulled off the toll road in South Bend, Marty glanced at his gas gauge. "Oh, no," he said. "I'm afraid I have to stop for gas. I'll try to make it quick."

They pulled into a gas station. To his driver's amazement, Father Ted greeted the attendant by name and began chatting with him in Spanish. Marty knew enough Spanish to make a rough translation. Father Ted was telling the man, "You really should sign up for continuing ed classes at Notre Dame. You're so smart; I know you'd have a lot to offer your classmates."

As they continued down US 31 Father Ted opened another envelope.

"Shall I drop you off at your residence or your office?" Marty asked.

"I've been up forty hours straight," admitted Father Ted, "but my mind is racing. Think I'd better tackle the pile of work in my office."

Two hours later, Father Hesburgh leaned back in his office chair and stretched. He put the memo he had just finished on the pile for his secretary to type up in the morning. Suddenly he heard a squeak outside on the fire escape, then a knock at the window. As he rose from his chair, he glanced at the clock. 3:35 a.m.

"Dave, good evening," he greeted the student. "Or should I say, good morning. How can I help you?"

"Hi, Father Ted. I saw your light on, so I knew I could come up and talk to you."

Father Ted motioned to two chairs. Dave sank into one with a deep sigh.

"I'm feeling all muddle-headed. For several months now I've been thinking I should change my major. But I'm a junior, and I'm afraid it's too late to switch now. If I went into pre-law instead of staying in business, I'd be in school at least an extra three years before I could start earning anything. I hate to ask my parents to finance that."

"Well, let's talk about it," Father Ted invited. "Why did you decide to major in business in the first place?"

Father Ted let Dave talk for a while, gently asking a

question from time to time. As he answered, Dave became less agitated and began thinking more objectively.

"Your reasons for going into law are pretty noble, Dave," Father Ted pointed out.

"I guess you're right, Father. I should aim for law school."

"You're the one who came to that conclusion, Dave. I just asked the right questions."

Dave was quiet for a minute, and then he said, "I didn't think of summer school as an option until our conversation tonight. I could try to get a job here in South Bend to help pay for law school. But I don't know where the rest of the money is going to come from."

"Well, let me see what I can do. Maybe there's a grant, or some money lying around in someone's office."

The student laughed.

Father Ted smiled to himself. He did have such an account "lying around"! When he gave speeches or served on corporate boards, he put that money aside to help individuals just like this young man.

"What do your parents think about all of this?" asked Father Hesburgh.

Dave looked down at the floor. "I haven't approached them yet," he admitted. "I wanted to have some kind of plan before I talked to them. I'll call them tomorrow."

As they both stood, Father Ted laughed, "No need to leave by the fire escape. I'm ready to call it a night. We can walk out the front door."

As Father Ted locked his office, Dave asked, "Father, can I ask about something I heard around campus?"

"Sure, fire away."

"Is it really true that the President of Notre Dame lives in two small rooms with a bathroom just like the other priests?

And that there are cans of orange juice and Campbell's soup stored in there?"

"Yep, that's the truth."

"And do you really sleep on an iron cot?"

"Yes, I do. And I sleep very well. I guess the scuttlebutt around campus got it right this time."

As they left the building, the sky was beginning to get light. Father Ted noticed the head custodian coming into work already.

"Hi," Father Ted said. "Dave, this is S.L. Montague. He keeps this plant running. I don't know what we'd do without him."

"Thanks, Father," said S.L.

"How's your work going?" Father Ted wanted to know. "And how's the family?"

S.L. grinned. "Fine thank you, Father. But I do believe if I had a real problem, you'd help me out."

"Of course I would," replied Father Ted.

As Dave and Father Ted walked down the steps of the main building, Dave said, "Father, thanks a lot. Maybe I can do something for you someday."

"You can do something right away, Dave. Pray for me every day."

"Will do, Father Ted." Dave started to walk away then another question popped into his head. "Father, where is your room?"

Father Ted smiled. "Just look for the dumpster, and my window is two floors above it. Luckily, I sleep so soundly I don't even hear the garbage truck in the morning."

When Father Ted got up the next day, he met the cleaning lady in the hall.

"Good morning, Mary. How's that boy of yours? I hope he's still getting good grades."

"Oh yes, Father," Mary answered. "His grades are way up there. My Jerry studies hard."

"That's good news. Tell him I'm looking forward to seeing him at Notre Dame in a few years. And, Mary, thanks for keeping this place sparkling."

Shortly after Father Ted got to his office, he took a phone call from Frank Freimann, CEO of Magnavox. "I have a young lady here who deserves a good education. I need you to take her under your wing."

Before Father Ted could tell him that was out of the question, Frank continued his story. "Her name is Hely Merle, and she's a distant cousin of mine. Like me, she was born in Austria. Her father disappeared after the Nazis sent him to Russia during the War. She and her mother wound up in a concentration camp, and Hely was only three when her mother died there. I'll take care of all her expenses, but she belongs at St. Mary's. I want you to come to Chicago and get her."

"All right, Frank," he answered, "but I didn't know being a foster father was part of my job description as President of Notre Dame."

When he first laid eyes on Hely, Father Ted could tell she hadn't had a mother's influence. She looked like a plucked chicken that hadn't learned anything about makeup.

"Are you a pretty good student?" he asked her.

"Oh, her grades at the orphanage were excellent, but she doesn't speak English," Frank interjected.

"What languages does she know?" Father Ted asked.

"Serbian, Croatian, German, and Russian," answered Frank.

"German's about my worst language," said Father Ted, "but that's all we have in common. Hopefully we can manage all right till she learns English. Did you bring a German-English dictionary, Hely?" he asked her.

"We're very lucky," he continued in halting German. "The day I called St. Mary's Academy about enrolling you, a student dropped out to go back to Mexico. So they have one bed open."

It took Hely only three months to learn enough English to enroll in St. Mary's College. But while she was at the Academy, Father Ted gained six more "children." It happened during a 1956 trip to South America.

Father Hesburgh's eyes traveled over the crowd at the American Embassy in Buenos Aires as he nibbled an hors d'oeuvre. He sighed. This cocktail party would postpone his search in Argentina for new Notre Dame teachers.

A voice from across the room interrupted Father Ted's musings. He saw an attractive woman bearing down on him. "You're the answer to my prayer!" she exclaimed.

"Victoria, please, you'll overwhelm him," her husband cautioned, touching her arm gently. "Father, allow us to introduce ourselves. I'm Charles O'Grady, and this is my wife Victoria."

Father Ted shook Mr. O'Grady's hand. "Father Ted Hesburgh," he said, "but you already seem to know who I am. Do you live in Argentina, or are you visitors like myself?"

"We're Americans," explained Charles, "but my business is here."

"That makes our six children Americans as well," continued Victoria, "but our son and five daughters have never even seen their own country."

"We think they ought to at least have a look, so we've decided to send them to Notre Dame and Saint Mary's for college," explained Charles.

"But they don't know many people in the States, and we can't afford to fly them back and forth all the time. That's why you're the answer to my prayer. I'm giving you my children to look after while they're at college," concluded Victoria.

When Anne and Virginia O'Grady arrived at St. Mary's

the next September, Father Ted arranged for them to room with Hely. Near the beginning of the semester, he took the three girls out to brunch at the Morris Inn. Before they even finished reading the menu, an alumnus spotted the president and came over to greet him.

"Hi, Bob. It's great to see you!" said Father Ted with a twinkle. "I'd like you to meet my daughters Hely, Anne, and Virginia. This is their first year at St. Mary's."

Bob raised his eyebrows. He knew priests were not allowed to marry, so how could Father Hesburgh have children? He excused himself and hastily backed away.

Father Ted smiled at the girls. "Well," he told them, "it would be easy for me to find out all kinds of things about you, but I don't plan to do any snooping. If you want me to know about your grades, your boyfriends, your problems, or whether you're going to Mass, you're going to have to tell me yourselves. Fair enough?"

"Sure," agreed the girls.

"I'll bet you can tell me a few things about life at St. Mary's that I don't learn from official sources," continued Father Ted. "Is it what you expected, or have you already had some surprises?" He leaned back and listened attentively as the girls told him about their first few days at college.

Anne and Virginia O'Grady became very good friends to Hely. This friendship helped her blossom. She was a good student and also good at music and dancing. Soon she was sewing all the costumes for plays at St. Mary's.

Like the O'Grady sisters, Hely found it easy to confide in Father Ted. He advised her on what to wear, and occasionally arranged dates for her. By the end of her sophomore year, Hely sought out Father Ted with news that couldn't wait.

"How about dinner at the Morris Inn tonight?" he suggested.

Hely sat at the table quite a while, nervously waiting for

Father Ted. The maître d' told her he had been delayed, but she didn't know what had happened.

When he finally slid into his seat, Father Ted apologized. "I'm so sorry I'm late," he explained. "As I was passing the desk, the clerk told me one of the guests had taken ill. I called a doctor and went up to the guest's room. I anointed him with the sacrament of the sick while we were waiting for help. Now tell me, what's going on with you?"

"I'm in love," Hely said. "I want to get married."

"Who's the lucky guy?" he asked her.

"Tony Shork. He's a senior at Notre Dame, headed for med school on a Woodrow Wilson Scholarship."

"Sounds pretty good, but I haven't met this young man," said Father Ted. "Let me see what I can find out."

As any parent would, Father Ted made some inquiries about his "daughter's" fiancé. Everyone spoke very highly of Tony, but Father Ted called the couple into his office.

"Don't you think you should wait a while, since you'll just be getting started in med school, Tony, and Hely is so young?"

They waited about eight months, until Christmas, then they invited Father Ted to witness their marriage vows.

This was the first of seven weddings Father Ted officiated for his "children." Before long, his "grandchildren" began arriving. By 1990, there were thirty of them, including three boys named Ted. When they became old enough to enroll at Notre Dame, Father Ted "fostered" another generation of college students.

One morning Father Ted answered a call from his brother Jim. After graduating from Notre Dame, Jim married and settled in South Bend. He and his growing family lived a short walk from campus.

"Hey, Ted," Jimmy said over the phone. "Can you come over for a cookout Saturday?"

"I'd love to. Let me double-check my calendar," Father Ted replied. "Wonderful. It looks clear!" He smiled to himself. He looked forward to those rare times when he could be just a favorite uncle for a few hours, not the president of the University of Notre Dame.

"Just a second," said Jimmy. "I'm going to put Mary on the phone."

"Uncle Ted," said Mary. "I'm inviting some friends over for my birthday party. You do know I'm going to be thirteen, right?"

"That's a momentous occasion," agreed Father Ted. "Anything I can do to make it special for you?"

"Well, I was hoping you could grill the hamburgers," Mary urged.

Saturday dawned warm and sunny, so Father Ted walked to Jimmy's house, but he had a hard time getting there on time. He knew the name of almost everyone he met on the path and stopped to say hi.

Finally he looked at his watch and quickened his pace.

When he arrived at his brother's house, Mary ran out to greet him. "Happy birthday, teenager," Father Ted said, kissing her on the cheek.

"Hurry up, Uncle Ted," she said. "My friends are starved for those hamburgers."

"Is that your favorite meal?" her uncle asked.

"You bet," answered Mary. "But I'm starting to like Chinese a lot too."

"I'll keep that in mind," said Father Ted. "Once you enroll at Notre Dame, I'll take you to South Bend's best Chinese restaurant."

"So glad we caught you in town," said Jim. "You travel so much, it can be hit or miss for the family. Are you off again soon?"

"No," answered Father Ted, flipping a burger. "I'll be here. I'm entertaining the Cardinal Archbishop of Paris on campus next week. I'd better brush up on my French."

So the next time Father Ted found himself taking a long walk across campus, he had a distinguished visitor along for a tour.

Seeing a gardener digging in the dirt, Father Ted greeted him by name. "The place looks great. Keep it up."

Then they passed a Chinese student. Father Hesburgh quickly switched from French to Chinese, asking, "How are you? Good, bad, or best?" Surprised and delighted, the student answered in Chinese, bowed slightly, and rushed away giggling.

At the Grotto, Father Hesburgh and his guest knelt down next to a jogger, sweaty from her run. As all three got up, Father Ted introduced the student to the Cardinal.

"Ask her why she stopped at the Grotto," the Cardinal asked in French. Father Ted translated the question.

The young lady looked puzzled. "I came to pray, of course. So many things to pray for these days."

Shaking his head, the Cardinal followed Father Ted to his office. "I am so impressed," he said. "In Europe I don't see this: young people who believe, young people who pray, young people full of idealism." (O'Brien p. 270)

The Cardinal picked up an ashtray of foreign coins from a table. "You are a numismatist then, Father?"

"I keep only enough coins from my travels to amuse the bored children whose parents bring them to my office."

"How kind you are." The Cardinal dug into his pocket and dropped a few French coins into the ashtray. "I will help you with your little guests."

Besides his family and staff, Father Ted also counted many members of the board of trustees as friends. He often spent Thanksgiving with Edmund Stephan's family in Chicago, where his Thanksgiving task was helping to make the gravy. He stood at the stove, smoking a cigar and stirring the gravy. Stephan watched anxiously, fearful cigar ashes might drop into the gravy, but they never did.

Working as hard as he did, both on and off-campus, took its toll on Father Ted, but he never thought about relaxing. One day in the mid-1950s, C.R. Smith, president of American Airlines and an adviser to Notre Dame's business school, cornered Father Ted at a party.

"You look terrible," he said bluntly. "You need a break, and I'm going to make sure you get one over Christmas vacation. How about going hunting and deep-sea fishing with me?"

"I love hunting and fishing," admitted Father Ted. "Where are we going?"

"Just leave that to me," replied C.R. "You don't mind if I invite Charlie Jones and his wife Jenny, do you?"

"That's fine with me," said Father Ted, "but are you sure it's all right with Charlie?"

Charlie did have a few doubts. He later confessed to Father Ted, "Here we were going to take a vacation and Smith just tells me with no warning that he's bringing a Catholic priest along. I figured you wouldn't drink, wouldn't smoke, wouldn't play cards, wouldn't fish, and wouldn't hunt. And I knew you wouldn't cuss like we did. You really surprised me. Except one thing—you never cussed."

Father Ted jokingly replied, "Well, nobody's perfect."

Soon Father Ted found himself in Rancho Las Cruces, Mexico, with C.R., Charlie, and Jenny.

Although religion played no official role in Mexico's government, Father Ted wore his clerical collar as usual. The people he met were thrilled to have a priest in their midst for the first time in forty years. People in the airport held out their hands for rosaries. The villagers begged him to say midnight Mass on Christmas Eve and New Year's Eve.

After two years, the townspeople built a small church on a cliff above the sea.

"Are you going to install stained-glass windows?" Father Hesburgh asked.

"Look out those windows," they invited him.

His eyes feasted on mountains, sea birds, and clouds.

"Isn't that better than stained glass?" they asked. "It's what God has made."

The four spent Christmas vacation in this peaceful place for fourteen years. After Charlie Jones died, Father Hesburgh continued to vacation with C.R. for sixteen more years, but not in a place with so many reminders of their friend.

Chapter Eleven

# A Tireless Warrior
# for Peace in Our Time

Father Hesburgh's telephone rang as he put a handwritten letter on a stack of mail for his secretary, Helen Hosinski, to type up in the morning. "Hello," he said.

"Father Hesburgh?"

"Speaking," replied Father Ted. It was a Sunday afternoon in 1954, and as usual he was in his office trying to get caught up.

"This is Sherman Adams, President Eisenhower's assistant. I'm calling to ask if you would accept an appointment to the National Science Board."

"Are you sure you've reached the right person?" asked Father Ted. "My training is in theology. I know nothing about science."

"That's why the President wants you," explained Adams. "He has twenty-three prominent scientists, but he needs someone on the Board with a moral perspective."

Father Hesburgh was quiet for a moment, then he said, "Well, if they can stand some philosophical and theological observations, I can certainly learn a great deal about science." (O'Brien p. 65)

He felt excited as he hung up the telephone. He knew scientists were exploring new areas every day, and he was eager to understand their work. Father Ted learned quickly from his voracious reading and through regular conversations with some of the world's greatest scientists. He served on the National Science Board for the next twelve years.

Father Ted admired the President. After leading the Allied troops to victory in World War II, General Dwight D. Eisenhower returned home a hero. "Ike" was easily elected President in 1952.

At that time, the United States and the Union of Soviet Socialist Republics (Russia and other countries that had been forcibly joined into a Communist nation) were locked in the Cold War. The two countries were suspicious of each other and fiercely competitive. Each wanted to extend its influence over other countries. Each wanted to be the first to send a person into space and to achieve other scientific breakthroughs. Each was busy developing more and more powerful nuclear weapons capable of destroying not only its rival but all the people in the world.

Eisenhower had the courage to question this. He knew that science could make new things possible, but he thought it was even more important to ask what's right and wrong. This was the perspective Father Hesburgh brought to the National Science Board. He raised fundamental questions, for example: What good is it to send up ten thousand satellites if we know nothing of the purpose of life and why we were placed on this earth in the first place?

Speaking at the United Nations in 1953, President Eisenhower urged all countries to stop building bombs and instead work together to harness nuclear energy for peaceful purposes such as electricity, medicine and farming. It took three years but, by 1956, the U.N. had almost finished a charter for this new, independent agency.

However, the two super-powers were far from agreeing whether the agency should have the right to inspect—to make sure atomic energy was being used peacefully, and not for weapons. U.S. Secretary of State John Foster Dulles thought a representative from the Catholic Church could effectively argue for these controls.

And so, in 1956, New York's Cardinal Spellman telephoned Father Hesburgh. "We need a Vatican representative to the International Atomic Energy Agency. Your service on the National Science Board means you're the person in the Catholic Church who probably knows the most about nuclear energy. Will you do it?"

Father Ted sighed. "Look," he objected, "I just got back from a trip to Latin America, and our fall semester is about to start. The last thing I want to do is pack up again and fly to New York to argue with the Russians for weeks!"

"The Church and the world need you," urged the Cardinal. "Besides, the conference is supposed to last seven weeks, but you don't have to be there the whole time. It's more of a symbolic role."

"All right," said Father Ted. "I'll do it. But I must be free to vote according to my conscience, without getting permission from some Church higher-up every time."

"I'll see what I can do," promised Spellman.

Not long after this conversation, Father Ted brought a cablegram to the credentials officer at the U.N. conference. It said the Vatican was giving him full power to sign any document as the Church's official representative.

The U.N. official shook his head in disbelief. "Nobody has that kind of power!" he exclaimed. He was used to delegates who had to check everything out with those who ruled their nation or organization.

For the first two weeks, Father Ted's seat sat empty much of the time. He would show up for the first few sessions and then fly back to Notre Dame, where he read the U.N. documents in his spare time.

One day when Father Ted was on hand, a Catholic observer at the U.N. cornered him. "Why are you hardly ever here?" he wanted to know.

"Look," answered Father Hesburgh, "I'm a very busy man. Cardinal Spellman told me I wouldn't have to show up very often."

The other man cleared his throat. "I'm afraid the Cardinal doesn't understand how things work at the U.N. If you're missing, the other delegates conclude you're not interested. Then even when you are there, they won't pay attention to what you have to say."

"Thanks for speaking up," Father Hesburgh said. "I'll rearrange my schedule."

During these meetings, Father Ted made an important friend. One day he sought out the Brazilian chairman.

"Ambassador Muñoz," Father Ted began, "Would you introduce me to one of the Russian delegates?"

"You want to befriend a Russian? Your countries don't get along!"

Father Ted shot back, "Just because our countries are hostile doesn't mean two individuals can't get to know each other better."

"Let me see," said the ambassador, running his finger down a list of delegates. "Vasily Emelyanov! He's a lot like you! He teaches science at a university and belongs to the Soviet Union's National Academy of Sciences. I'll introduce you."

Although the two men had to depend on a translator,

they hit it off very well. After that, they looked for each other at every social event. But something puzzled Emelyanov.

"Father Ted, we can be in the middle of a group of people chatting amiably, but as soon as a news photographer comes along, all the Americans scatter. All but you. Why are they afraid to be photographed with me?"

"Let's see if I can explain," Father Ted began. "There's a lot of anti-Communist feeling in our country right now. The other Americans are afraid if they're seen talking with a Russian, Senator Joe McCarthy will stand up in the Senate and accuse them of being Communists."

"What about you?" Emelyanov persisted.

"Oh, I'm not afraid of him," explained Father Ted. "You see, I don't work for the American government. I work for the Pope in Rome."

Emelyanov roared with laughter.

On a Monday, the charter of the International Atomic Energy Agency was due to come up for a vote.

The Swiss ambassador appealed to Father Ted. "The European delegates are afraid the section on inspection isn't going to pass. Most delegates won't agree to let the agency visit nuclear plants inside their countries. But otherwise how can the U.N. be sure nuclear energy is being used for peaceful purposes and not to make weapons? We're counting on you. Write a good talk and give it just before the vote; maybe it will help us win," he said.

"I can't," explained Father Ted. "I have to be in Washington, D.C., for a meeting of the National Science Board that day."

"What are we going to do?" the ambassador worried. "Can you be on standby? If the vote looks very close, I'll call Monday morning, and you can fly to the U.N. in New York City to make that speech."

Sure enough, around noon the Swiss ambassador called, "Father Hesburgh, you need to get here and give that talk." So Father Ted hopped into a taxi and got on the shuttle flight to New York.

Everything was going fine until the captain came over the loudspeaker: "Ladies and gentlemen, this is your pilot. I regret to inform you that our plane has lost an engine. You are not in any danger, but we'll have to turn back to D.C."

Father Ted groaned. Minor inconveniences had often changed his travel plans but this was different. He had to get to the United Nations in time to give that speech!

By the time Father Hesburgh boarded another plane, an hour had been lost. Could he get there in time?

He had written a talk on the flight to Washington that morning, but he wasn't quite satisfied with it. Then he glanced over and realized that his seatmate on the shuttle was Harold Stassen, the U.S. representative for disarmament. Stassen helped Father Hesburgh improve his talk.

As soon as they landed, Father Ted jumped into another cab.

"To the U.N. right away!" he exclaimed.

As the cab pulled up, he hoped the U.N. guards recognized him. No time to show his ID!

Completely out of breath, Father Ted plopped into his chair in the assembly hall. Just then a voice came over the public-address system announcing "the delegate for the Vatican."

His talk was very well received, and the delegates voted in favor of inspection, a decision that is still important as additional nations attempt to develop nuclear weapons.

Once the treaty was signed, Father Ted hoped his work was done. No such luck! Instead, the Catholic Church asked him to be one of its two permanent delegates to the

International Atomic Energy Agency. He served for fifteen years. During that time the agency produced the Nuclear Nonproliferation Treaty preventing additional countries from developing nuclear weapons.

The International Atomic Energy Agency held its meetings in Vienna, Austria. Each delegation hosted social events, usually dances and cocktail parties. But Father Hesburgh had a different idea. What if all the delegates could pray together?

After talking it over with Frank Folsom, the other Vatican delegate, he invited everyone to Sunday Mass, followed by a nice brunch.

"Wonder what kind of turnout we'll get," mused Frank.

"Hard to tell," replied Father Ted. "Of course these delegates practice many different world religions, and those from the Soviet bloc don't believe in God at all. On the other hand, they know and respect us, and this is something novel. I don't know what to expect."

"Where shall we hold the Mass?" asked Frank.

"I have my eye on Karlskirche. It's a beautiful church, right in the middle of Vienna, but it's pretty small, so a modest turnout won't be too embarrassing. I'm hoping the Archbishop will celebrate the Mass."

Reluctantly, Archbishop Franz Koenig agreed. "Can you read the Gospel in all the official languages of the conference?" Father Ted asked. "And of course German, since we're in Vienna."

"Remind me what those languages are," said the Archbishop.

"French, English, Spanish, and Russian," replied Father Ted.

"Why bother with Russian?" Koenig asked. "The Russians won't even be there."

"I think they will," said Father Ted.

"They never come to church," objected the Archbishop, "I've been living here with them for ten years, and they've never been inside the church, except maybe to look around. They're atheists. Don't you know that?"

Finally Father Ted got him to agree to read the Gospel in Russian if the Soviet delegates showed up.

Ten minutes before Mass, the church was empty. Father Ted peeked nervously out the sacristy door. "Come, Holy Spirit!" he prayed.

Then the ambassador from India arrived, followed by the Muslim ambassador from Pakistan. In a few minutes, the church was packed, including the Russians. This Mass became an annual tradition, and everyone looked forward to it.

Because of his honesty and respect for all the delegates, Father Hesburgh had many opportunities to be a reconciler. A dramatic one occurred in 1958 during a round of speeches in Vienna. By then Emelyanov was head of the Soviet delegation. Just before he was scheduled to speak, an American got up to brag.

"The United States has just given the agency two mobile radioisotope units. They'll only be parked outside for a few more minutes if anyone wants to go see them," he invited. Sure enough, almost everyone left the hall to have a look.

Predictably, Emelyanov was furious when he looked out on a nearly empty auditorium. He lit into the United States, sharply criticizing it for a whole list of things.

This speech in turn upset John McCone, head of the U.S. Atomic Energy Commission. He told the U.S. delegates and their European allies to boycott the Russian cocktail party that night.

"Calm down, John," Father Ted told him. "Delegates always exaggerate. Emelyanov didn't mean three quarters of it.

He just had to score points with the politicians back home. Besides, he had every reason to be upset with us. We can't let such a little thing shut down the lines of communication between the major nuclear powers."

McCone folded his arms across his chest and glared. So Father Hesburgh was the only American who attended the cocktail party. As he went through the receiving line, Emelyanov said, "I have to talk with you privately."

Father Ted stepped aside with his friend, who continued, "The Russians have no idea why so few people have come to our party."

"You asked for it," Father Ted retorted.

Emelyanov was surprised. "My people told me it was a very good speech," he said.

"Your people have to tell you that because they work for you. But I am your friend, and I am telling you it was a very bad speech." Father Hesburgh continued, "Sure, we Americans are to blame for some things, but not everything! Insults like that might even start a nuclear war. I know you don't want to destroy the world so your grandchildren can't enjoy it."

"OK," said Emelyanov. "You tell me what to do, and I'll do it."

"Before the end of this conference," Father Ted told him, "you and McCone have to sit down together and make things right between you."

Neither man wanted to do this, but Father Ted persuaded both that it was essential. He set up a meeting in the parlor of his hotel room at 9 a.m. Sunday morning.

When they arrived with their translators, both men were scowling. To break the tension, Father Ted adopted a mysterious tone, "Gentlemen, I have something behind this screen that you might find interesting," he invited.

Both approached gingerly, as if expecting a booby trap,

but all they found behind the red screen was the little table on which Father Hesburgh often said Mass. It was covered with an altar cloth with Old Russian writing all over it.

"What's this all about?" asked McCone.

"This kind of altar cloth was developed during World War II," Father Ted explained. "A priest used to need a consecrated altar stone in order to celebrate Mass. But when chaplains parachuted out of planes, that stone whacked too many of them on the head. A cloth like this was much safer.

"I don't know much Russian," Father Ted admitted. "Vasily, can you translate what's written here?"

The two men bent over the altar cloth as Emelyanov translated. "Matthew, Mark, Luke, and John. Right?" Father Ted nodded. "In the name of the Father and the Son and the Holy Spirit. Right?"

"Right," agreed Father Ted.

"It says this is the crucifixion, and these are Mary, John, and Jesus, and this antimensium was consecrated for Father Hesburgh by Bishop Elko. Right?"

"Right," said Father Ted. "Good for you."

"I studied the Old Russian as a boy," Emelyanov explained.

"Aren't you surprised that I say Mass every day over a Russian cloth?" Father Ted asked. Both men grinned.

"I'm going to leave you gentlemen alone now," said Father Ted. "Your meeting is absolutely private. No one will interrupt you or record what you say. We'll lock these doors as we leave so no one else can get in, and the phone is off the hook. We've left you pads, pencils, and pitchers of water in case you need them."

As Father Ted started to leave, McCone said, "I'll see you at Mass at eleven o'clock."

Emelyanov quickly chimed in, "I, too, will see you at Mass at eleven o'clock."

The two delegates spent the next two hours alone together. Father Ted waited for them in the hotel lobby as long as he could, but finally he headed over to Karlskirche. At eleven o'clock, neither man had arrived for Mass.

Father Ted couldn't help being nervous. He headed into the sacristy where the Archbishop was about to begin the entrance procession.

"Look, Your Eminence," Father Ted said, "we're expecting an American ambassador and a Russian ambassador, and we want to put them up in the sanctuary because it is a very special day. I'll tell you all about that later, but could you delay starting Mass until I give you the signal?"

The Archbishop had been through this sort of thing with Father Ted before. He simply said, "No problem."

Finally John McCone and his wife walked in. As Father Ted escorted them up the aisle, John admitted, "You were right. He is a good person. We buried all the nonsense, and we made some important plans for the future."

By the time Father Ted walked back down the aisle, Emelyanov had arrived. Father Ted seated him next to McCone. As they turned and smiled at each other, everyone in the church breathed a sigh of relief.

About a year later, these two men were the top aides for an important meeting between President Eisenhower and Soviet Prime Minister Nikita Khrushchev.

Sometimes Father Hesburgh was criticized for spending so much time away from Notre Dame. A favorite joke asked:

"What's the difference between God and Father Hesburgh?"

"God is everywhere. Father Hesburgh is everywhere but Notre Dame."

One year when he chose to attend a meeting in Vienna instead of showing up at Notre Dame's freshman orientation, someone made a negative comment. A student defended Father Hesburgh. "It's foolish to request that he neglect the millions of poor and hungry in the world in order to please a handful of white, upper middle-class, well-fed parents." (O'Brien p. 168)

Chapter Twelve

# Our Civil Rights Situation Was Abominable

O ne day around 1960, Father Hesburgh was waiting for the South Shore train to take him from Chicago back to South Bend. A black woman was standing a little way down the platform, so he walked over and struck up a conversation with her. After they chatted a while, she told him, "This last week I was giving my four-year-old son a bath. Of course I told him, 'Scrub hard with the soap,' and do you know what he asked me?"

Shaking his head, Father Ted replied, "I have no idea."

"He looked up at me with those big eyes and said, 'Mommy, if I scrub myself hard enough, will I be white?'"

"And what did you tell him?" Father Ted asked.

"I said, 'No, you're colored and you'll always be colored.' Then he let out a deep sigh and told me, 'It's better to be white.'"

"Did you let him get away with that?" Father Ted wanted to know.

The black woman turned and looked at him long and hard. "Why shouldn't I? Isn't it better to be white in America?"

Father Ted was disturbed by her reply. "It may seem better," he began, "but that's not the way a youngster should think. He has his whole life ahead of him! What is today doesn't always have to be. Please, God! It won't be that way forever in our nation." (O'Brien p. 80)

Father Ted watched people board the train. The black lady walked to the back of the train to sit with the other black passengers. Father Ted would have been happy to sit beside her, but he didn't want to make her feel uncomfortable all the way home. So he took a seat in the front near the other white people. Because they were on a train in the northern part of the country, there was no law forbidding them to sit in the same section, yet almost no one crossed those customary barriers.

Father Ted hadn't known a single black person growing up in Syracuse, and there were only a handful of Africans in his classes in Rome. Finally while he was studying for his doctorate in Washington, D.C., he spent time working and talking with interracial groups. That's when he began to have a passion for civil rights.

That passion grew naturally out of his Christian faith. "God draws no color line when He comes to dwell through grace in the souls of men. What's good enough [for] Him should be good enough for us." (O'Brien p. 77)

The train pulled out of the station toward Notre Dame, where Father Ted knew there were only a handful of black students. The first three graduated in 1947. Father Ted smiled to himself as he thought about George R. Rhodes, Jr., who earned a master's degree in education in 1950. George was a fine man who went on to earn a Ph.D. and become a principal. But then Father Ted sighed. He knew that throughout the Southern states, black people were not allowed to enroll in state universities or study alongside white people to be doctors or lawyers. They could only go to Howard or Meharry, schools exclusively for African-Americans. He hoped his commission could change that inequity soon.

Three years earlier, in 1957, President Eisenhower called on Father Ted. "I need you on the brand-new Civil Rights Commission."

"What's our mandate, Mr. President?" Father Ted wanted to know.

"You're to find out whether black citizens are being denied their rights."

Father Ted was thrilled. Civil rights for black Americans were very much on his heart—and here was a chance to do something about it!

But he had a few more questions for the President. "How is this going to work? Whom else are you appointing to the commission?"

The President sighed. "It's a balancing act," he admitted as he gave Father Ted the names. Father Ted whistled.

As he hung up the telephone, he counted. Among the six commissioners, there were three Northerners and three Southerners, five whites and one black man, three Democrats, two Republicans—and Father Ted, an independent. He realized they would have to do a lot of patient negotiation.

Father Ted headed to Washington, D.C., where each commissioner had to appear in front of the Senate Judiciary Committee before the whole Senate voted whether to confirm him. The Senator from Mississippi leaned over, the end of his big cigar inches from Father Ted's face. He repeatedly blew a big puff of cigar smoke and asked one hostile question after another. However, the full Senate voted to confirm all six commissioners. They were sworn in at the White House on January 2, 1958.

Afterward they went to look at their office in a building across from the White House. The only room large enough to hold six people was filthy. Its black and white floor tile made Father Ted feel like he was in a public men's room.

"What's that heap of unopened mail spilling off the table?" he wondered aloud.

J. Ernest Wilkins, Undersecretary of Labor and the only black commissioner, picked up an envelope, tore it open, and skimmed it. "Looks like a civil rights complaint," he said.

"Do we have secretaries to keep track of all this?" asked former Florida governor Doyle Carlton.

"Afraid not," answered John Hannah, president of Michigan State University. "Congress created our commission, but they didn't appropriate any money for it. I hear Eisenhower's trying to tap an emergency fund to get us started."

"God bless him," said Father Ted.

John Battle, former governor of Virginia, said. "We have less than two years to finish our fact-finding and make recommendations to the President and Congress. And we don't have any power to enforce what we recommend."

"But we do have one powerful tool," Robert Storey, dean of Southern Methodist Law School, reminded them. "We can use the subpoena to obtain official records, require witnesses to testify in court, and protect black witnesses."

"Otherwise," noted Father Hesburgh, "none of them would be willing to tell us their stories. Why should they subject themselves and their families to being harassed or even killed by irate whites?"

"So much to do, so little time," said John Hannah, commission chairman. "Where shall we start?"

After a long discussion, they decided to zero in on voting. That was the issue that had deadlocked Congress. Congress couldn't agree on whether black citizens needed more laws to help them exercise their right to vote.

"So," suggested Father Hesburgh, "let's investigate

whether qualified black people can in fact register and vote in the South today."

The commission planned to hold its first hearings in Montgomery, Alabama, the first capital of the Confederacy. They set a date and wrote ahead for hotel reservations.

Because one commissioner was black and two black lawyers were on the staff, every hotel in Montgomery turned them down.

"Sorry, gentlemen, it's against Alabama law for Negroes and whites to stay in the same hotel," read one polite letter after another.

In fact, "niggers" were not allowed to mix with white people anywhere in the South before 1964. They could not attend the same schools, live in the same neighborhoods, use the same drinking fountains, sit at the same lunch counters, or even be buried in the same cemeteries. Signs posted on restaurants, public toilets, drugstores, and beaches stated: WHITES ONLY.

"There's always Maxwell Air Force Base," suggested Robert Storey.

"I know the commanding officer," said John Hannah. "I'll write to him today and request accommodations in the Bachelor Officer Quarters."

The major who answered his letter was very apologetic. "Sorry, we can't possibly house Negroes and whites together. The good people of Montgomery would never stand for it."

Father Ted couldn't believe it. "Don't they know President Truman integrated all the armed forces ten years ago?"

John Hannah fumed, but he went up the chain of command. He complained, but the Secretary of the Air Force didn't want to go over the head of the local commander, and the Secretary of Defense didn't want to reverse an order given by the Secretary of the Air Force.

Finally John Hannah said, "Guess we'll have to go all the way to the top this time. No more letters. I'm calling Ike."

After Hannah explained the situation to the President, the other commissioners could hear his angry response. Later Father Ted remembered, "Ike blew a fuse. He was no great liberal, but he was a fair man. He sat down and wrote a scathing executive order to the general at Maxwell, saying that the members of the commission would indeed be accommodated there." First hurdle overcome.

Even though the Fifteenth Amendment to the Constitution had given black men the right to vote in 1870, the commission discovered that not a single black person in Montgomery County, Alabama, was registered to vote. White voting registrars in the city, many of them high school dropouts, made it impossible for black people to register to vote—even those who were doctors, lawyers, or professors.

During their hearings the commission heard one horror story after another. One potential voter was turned down because of what the registrar recorded as a "spilling" error on his application. Another was asked to demonstrate that he knew how to read. The registrar handed him a Chinese newspaper and asked what it said. With amazingly good humor, he responded, "I guess it says I'm not going to vote."

The story in Texas, Georgia, and Mississippi was the same. Black people were routinely denied the right to vote on flimsy pretexts.

At one hearing, Father Ted asked a black teacher why she wanted to vote.

She answered, "I have a master's degree in biology. I'm a teacher at the university, and my husband is a Ph.D. When the last presidential election came up, one of my four children asked me if I was going to vote. I said, 'I can't. I'm black and they won't let me.' My child said, 'That's not right.'"

She continued, "That's when I knew I couldn't hope to teach my children about democracy if I could not vote, and they knew I could not vote."

In Louisiana, a black dentist explained that he had shown the registrar his photo ID, a driver's license, a copy of his federal income tax return, his certification as a dentist, his membership card in the national professional dental society, and his honorable discharge as a Captain from the U.S. Army. He told the official, "I am an American citizen as much as you are, and I intend to vote."

The registrar looked him up and down. "Sorry, boy," he said. "You'll need to produce two registered voters to vouch for you."

"You know that's impossible," muttered the dentist. "There's not a single black on the voter rolls, and no white voter would dare stand up for me."

When the dentist told the commission this story, Father Ted said, "Captain, I believe you. I want you to go back to that registration place tomorrow morning and tell them that you testified at this hearing. I am sure they will already know it because they are undoubtedly watching us on television right now. If they don't register you, call me immediately and let me know. I will then call the President of the United States, who was the top general in the U.S. Army, and I will tell him that one of his officers is being prevented from voting in Louisiana. I can promise you that the President will make things so hot for everyone that they will wish they had never heard of you."

The next day, the dentist registered to vote for the first time.

Just before the commission's two-year term ended, they scheduled a final public hearing in Shreveport, Louisiana. They had spent three months and thirty thousand dollars preparing for that hearing, but before they could begin, a federal marshal marched into the courtroom and announced, "You are enjoined from holding your hearing because the Civil Rights Commission is unconstitutional."

At a future date, this challenge was overturned by the U.S. Supreme Court, but at that moment the commission members were stymied. They had to close their briefcases and return to their lodgings.

Discouraged, they sank into chairs in the common room of the airbase where they were staying. It was swelteringly hot, the food was awful, and noisy jets made it hard to sleep or even think. How could they possibly start writing the report the President and Congress were expecting in a month?

Suddenly Father Ted had a great idea. "We have no reason to stay in Shreveport," he pointed out. "Let's move to Notre Dame's retreat center at Land O'Lakes, Wisconsin. That will be a much more pleasant place to work!"

One phone call got someone started stocking the comfortable lodge with supplies and refreshments. Another located a benefactor willing to fly them to the cool, fresh air of Wisconsin in a private plane. Soon they left Shreveport far behind.

Preliminary findings and conclusions had already been written after they finished hearings in each city, but the commission needed to make its final recommendations. Father Ted and the staff sat in the back of the plane to draft these resolutions. But Father Ted was apprehensive. Was there any chance that all six commissioners would agree to them?

As they sat around the table at Land O'Lakes that evening enjoying steaks and drinks, they made an important discovery: every one of them was an enthusiastic fisherman.

"Let's go out on the lake and fish," Father Ted proposed. He shot up a quick silent prayer to the Holy Spirit. "I know this is an unusual request, but it would be very helpful if each one of these guys caught some fish."

Sure enough, they all caught fish—a lot of fish, mostly bass and walleye. "I can't wait to have these for breakfast!" Father Ted exclaimed.

As a big, bright moon rose over the lake, they gathered around a large table on the screened porch. The staff and Father Hesburgh brought out their twelve recommendations and put them to a vote. Mellow from the pleasant evening of fishing, the commissioners unanimously agreed to eleven of the recommendations. The twelfth, on integrating education, passed 5-1.

By the next morning, some of the commissioners were having second thoughts. Had they been bewitched by the moonlight? But they were men of honor who wouldn't go back on their word.

When they presented the report to President Eisenhower, he was amazed. "How did six people with such diverse backgrounds and opinions come to such substantial agreement?" he wondered aloud.

Father Ted smiled. "Sir, you didn't just appoint Democrats and Republicans, Northerners and Southerners. What you did was appoint six fishermen."

With a twinkle, President Eisenhower replied, "Then we've got to put more fishermen on commissions and have more reports written at Land O'Lakes, Wisconsin."

The commission kept being renewed two years at a time under the direction of several different Presidents of the United States. Besides voting rights, they investigated employment, housing, education, the courts, and the right to be in public places like stores, theaters, and restaurants.

This was such demanding work that from time to time commissioners resigned and were replaced. But it was so dear to Father Hesburgh's heart that he stayed on, serving on the Civil Rights Commission for a total of fifteen years.

In 1964, a monumental piece of legislation addressed many of the abuses exposed by the Civil Rights Commission. President Lyndon Johnson, a proud Southerner from Texas, presented the Omnibus Civil Rights Act before a joint session of Congress. In Father Hesburgh's words, "Without Lyndon Johnson's courage and vision upon taking office, we would not have come as far as we have today on civil rights and human rights."

A day after the Omnibus Civil Rights Act went into effect, two black lawyers with the commission decided to test it. They checked into a motel in Jackson, Mississippi; no one objected. They ate at the best restaurant in town; there were surprised looks, but no one threw them out. Then they went to a movie, where they sat on the main floor instead of the balcony formerly reserved for black people; no one complained. A day earlier, they would have been barred from all these places. Now they walked into all of them without incident.

After eleven years on the commission, Father Ted was tired. He asked the new President, Richard Nixon, to accept his resignation. Instead, Nixon asked him to serve as chairman. Father Ted agreed. The commission turned its attention to civil rights abuses within the federal government. Their investigation showed that the government wasn't following its own policies with regard to civil rights.

When President Nixon discovered that the study reflected badly on his administration, he asked the commission to delay publication until after the 1972 election. Father Hesburgh refused. Nixon was re-elected in spite of the report. One of the first things he did after the election was to fire Father Hesburgh from the commission.

Once he got over being upset, Father Ted breathed a sigh

of relief. In those fifteen years, he had fought and won many battles on behalf of racial justice and civil rights.

His commission papers are now filed at Notre Dame Law School's Center for Civil and Human Rights, jokingly known for a time as "The Civil Rights Commission in Exile."

Back at Notre Dame between commission hearings, something bothered Father Ted. Eleven percent of the population in South Bend was African-American, yet there were only forty-five black people working on the campus at the University of Notre Dame! Beginning in the fall of 1967, Father Hesburgh directed that at least eleven percent of the people working for Notre Dame be minorities. Within four years, 345 minority persons were employed at the university.

President Hesburgh also used his contacts and influence to secure funding for scholarships for minority students. He himself recruited academically excellent, minority high school students to come to Notre Dame, and he directed Notre Dame alumni clubs all over the country to do the same. In the spring of 1969 he gave the campus Afro-American Society eighteen thousand dollars to organize a Black Culture Week.

Father Hesburgh would be the first to say how much work remains to be done in the field of full rights for Americans of every race and religion. However, sweeping changes have occurred in the civil rights landscape of this country in the past fifty years. When Father Ted began his work on the commission, Barack Obama's parents could not have legally married or made their home in many of our states. It was a great personal satisfaction for Father Theodore Hesburgh to see this black man elected President of the United States on November 4, 2008.

When President Obama addressed the Notre Dame graduates the following May, Father Hesburgh sat behind the students. He stood and waved when Notre Dame presented a special gift to the President—a framed photo of Hesburgh, arm-in-arm with Martin Luther King, Jr., at a 1964 civil rights rally. In his talk, President Obama honored Father Ted at length for his work in promoting civil rights in this country.

Chapter Thirteen

# One Person Can Make a Difference

S hortly after the 1961 inauguration of President John Fitzgerald Kennedy, Father Hesburgh was in Washington, D.C., on Civil Rights Commission business. As he strode across Lafayette Park, Father Ted couldn't help sense the excitement in the air.

Lines from Kennedy's inaugural address replayed themselves in Father Ted's head. Kennedy urged people all over the world to come together to fight "the common enemies of man: tyranny, poverty, disease and war itself. And so, my fellow Americans, ask not what your country can do for you—ask what you can do for your country."

As he glanced at the White House lawn across the street, Father Ted caught sight of two men excitedly waving a piece of paper in the air. They seemed to be trying to get his attention. Shading his eyes in the sunlight, he made out Sargent Shriver, Kennedy's brother-in-law, and attorney Harris Wofford, who had left the Civil Rights Commission to work on Kennedy's election campaign.

He sprinted across the street. "What have you got there?" he wanted to know.

"It's Kennedy's executive order starting the Peace Corps," they explained. "We knew you'd be happy to know it's moving forward."

"I'm glad he's following up on that campaign promise," agreed Father Ted.

Kennedy envisioned the Peace Corps as "a pool of trained men and women sent overseas to help foreign countries meet their urgent needs for skilled manpower" such as teachers, farmers and healthcare workers. These volunteers were to spend two years living like the people where they were sent, doing the same work, eating the same simple food, and using their ingenuity to figure out how to make people's everyday lives better.

A few hours later, Father Ted was back at Notre Dame when his phone rang. It was Shriver and Wofford.

"The President wants us to come up with a pilot program so we can try out the Peace Corps idea," Shriver explained.

Wofford continued, "You have so many connections all around the world, we thought you might be able to help us."

Father Ted grinned. "I certainly can," he answered. "You can have your pick: Bangladesh, Uganda or Chile. Which do you like?"

The two men were silent a moment. "Let's start with Chile," Shriver suggested.

The next day, Father Hesburgh got together a group of people at Notre Dame who knew a lot about Latin America.

"I've got an idea for a project," suggested Father Ted. "Why couldn't we use radio to teach people in the inaccessible central valley of Chile how to read and write?" The experts kicked around the idea for a while and decided Father Ted should write up the proposal and send it to Shriver.

"I'll get right on it," he promised. "Sounded like they were in a big hurry." However, he heard nothing from the White House for five or six weeks.

Finally he took a phone call from Shriver. "We have to get moving right away," he told Father Ted. "We like your project, and we'd like you to go down there and get the Chilean government to approve it. Of course, we can't do anything unless their government invites us to do it."

"I understand," agreed Father Ted. "I'll book a flight to Santiago as soon as possible."

Shriver cleared his throat. "There's one other thing," he said.

"What's that?" Father Ted wanted to know.

"I've been getting a lot of flak from people who are a little sensitive about the fact that Kennedy is our first Catholic President and this project seems to be spearheaded by a Catholic university. Is there any way you could get sponsorship from a broader group?"

Father Ted thought for a minute. "I'll check with the Indiana Conference of Higher Education," he promised. "That's all the colleges in Indiana. I'm sure that will be diverse enough for your critics." The group that flew to Chile's capital with Father Ted wound up including representatives from Yale as well as Indiana University.

After a few days in Chile, Father Ted was discouraged. Not one college or radio station wanted to get involved.

"What now?" IU's Peter Frankel asked Father Ted.

"I've been hearing about something that's already in existence. Maybe we can build on their Institute for Rural Education," Father Ted suggested.

"What's that?" asked Frankel.

"As I understand it, these private schools teach children

who live out in the country about farming, healthy eating and good hygiene. What if we put our Peace Corps volunteers to work in schools like that?"

Frankel tapped his pencil thoughtfully on his clipboard. "So how many agencies would need to approve that?" he asked.

"I think we need to talk with three key people: the Minister of Education, the Minister of Agriculture, and Julio Philippe," Father Ted answered.

"Philippe, Philippe. Why does his name keep coming up?" asked Frankel.

"He's the assistant to the President of Chile. We won't be able to get anywhere without his help."

"I suppose we'll have to go through the American Embassy to set up appointments with those people," said the dean of the Yale Law School. He picked up the phone immediately, but two days later, nothing had happened. The only meeting the Embassy had been able to arrange had fallen through.

"You've got to do something," Father Ted told their contact at the Embassy. "We're here on behalf of the President of the United States, and we're scheduled to fly back home in two days. We can't go without at least presenting our ideas to the government!"

"I'm very sorry, Father. I just can't help you."

Suddenly an idea popped into Father Ted's head. Father Mark McGrath! Besides being dean of Catholic University in Santiago, he was a Holy Cross priest!

"I'll see what I can do," Father McGrath promised. "I happen to know both of those ministers, and Julio Philippe is a good friend of mine."

"I've got good news and bad news," Father McGrath said when he called back. "The good news is that you have an appointment with Julio Philippe. The bad news is that he can only meet with you for ten minutes."

"I'll talk fast," said Father Ted.

Ten minutes into the meeting, Julio Philippe got excited. "That's the best program I've ever heard of!" he exclaimed. "Tell me more." He asked so many questions that the meeting lasted an hour and a half. He promised that the President of Chile would approve the plan as soon as they sent him a copy in writing.

Father Hesburgh flew back to the States and wrote up the proposal. Next he needed signatures from people in the American government. "Can you walk this from desk to desk for me?" he asked Harris Wofford.

"Sure, I'll sign this," said an official at the U.S. State Department, "but what's the rush? It will take months before you hear back from the government of Chile." In the next two days, he and a dozen other people put their signatures on the document creating the first project of the Peace Corps, but most were skeptical.

"You'll never get this project off the ground," they said. "You know how it is with Latin American governments. They always say they'll do it mañana (tomorrow)."

Father Ted cabled the agreement to Julio Philippe at 1 p.m. on a Thursday afternoon, just before the beginning of a three-day weekend in Chile. By 3 p.m. that same day, they had their answer. "Send your volunteers down whenever you are ready," cabled Philippe, on behalf of the President of Chile.

The first 45 volunteers came from all over the United States. They spent a summer at Notre Dame training for their service with the Peace Corps. Father Hesburgh personally welcomed them to their first meeting.

"I'm so glad you're here," he said over and over. "You're going to improve so many people's lives!"

"Do you know Spanish?" he asked one of the volunteers.

"Afraid not," Tom answered.

"I don't know much either," admitted Father Ted. "Let me see your schedule. I plan to sit in on as many classes as I can."

"We're having a picnic Friday afternoon. Hope you can join us," another student invited. "Do you play soccer? I've been told that's a sure ticket for getting to know kids in Chile."

"I'm not very good," said Father Ted, "but I'd be happy to scrimmage with you. Don't forget, the game we call soccer is known as football in the rest of the world."

At the end of the summer, these young people began their assignments in Chile. Father Ted did his best to keep in touch with them, but he wanted to see their work firsthand. In March he called Sargent Shriver with a request.

"Sarge, I'm planning to spend Easter week in Chile. I know President Kennedy's very busy, but could you get him to write a letter of thanks for me to take to the volunteers? It would mean a lot to them."

"Sure," agreed Shriver. "When do you need it?"

A large manila envelope arrived on Father Ted's desk just before he was scheduled to fly to Chile that Easter of 1962. He hurriedly put it in his briefcase, planning to make a copy for each volunteer once he reached Santiago.

After the plane took off from Chicago, Father Ted pulled out the envelope. To his amazement, the President had addressed a personal letter on White House stationery to each volunteer, signed "Jack Kennedy."

When he landed in Santiago, the professor heading the Peace Corps project met him at the airport. "Hi, Walter," Father Ted greeted him. "I hope you've been able to arrange my itinerary to visit all 45 volunteers. I have something very special to give them."

"Father Ted," objected Walter Langford, "I know you want to see each one, but they're spread over 800 miles. It would take at least a month to get around to each remote station. I've drawn up a route that will give you a good taste of the work they're doing in the seven days you have. But you'd better rest up from your trip first."

"I insist on seeing every single volunteer," declared Father Ted. "And I'm ready to get started as soon as you are."

During the next week, he traveled by plane, train, bus, jeep and on foot, with little time to rest and no opportunity to shower. But Father Ted managed to see every volunteer at his station.

"How's attendance at your school?" Father Ted asked two young women.

"Better now," said one. "It took us a while to figure out why half our students were absent each day, but finally one of them admitted that they were plagued with diarrhea. We started scrubbing down the school kitchen, putting up flypaper, and making sure they used hot water to wash the dishes."

"And throwing out spoiled meat and produce," added the other. "Food was being delivered at the end of every day, and we realized it was the spoiled leftovers. Instead, we began driving a pickup truck to the market first thing in the morning to buy fresh produce."

"I'll bet that made a big difference," offered Father Ted.

"You bet. Now our students are almost never sick. Once the ladies working in the kitchen realized what a difference it made, they changed the way they handle the food."

"What's your assignment, Tom?" Father Ted asked another volunteer.

"I'm supposed to be setting up agricultural cooperatives," Tom Scanlon answered. "Me!"

"And why not?" Father Ted wanted to know.

"Well," answered Tom, "I may have a Master's degree, but I hardly knew a horse from a cow when I got here. I've had to learn on the job. But I have a big challenge ahead of me now."

"What's that?" Father Ted asked.

Tom sighed. "There are some very poor people on top of a mountain who are suffering from yaws."

Father Ted shuddered. "That's a tropical infection that eats into skin and bone, isn't it? Something we can easily treat these days with penicillin."

"Yes," agreed Tom, "but first we need to get permission from the Communist leader of the village. When I climbed up the mountain to introduce myself and ask if I could bring a nurse back to treat the sick people, he sneered at me. 'You'll have to come back in July,' he told me. I said, 'Sure, we'll be back'—but then I realized that July is the middle of winter in Chile!"

"What are you going to do about it?" asked Father Ted.

"We'll just have to bring the penicillin up that mountain in the snow," said Tom.

Father Ted later learned that Tom kept his promise. He and the nurse rode up the mountain as far as their horses would take them. When the snow was up to the horses' bellies, the two volunteers got off and pulled the horses the rest of the way up. Amazed, the Communist leader let them treat the villagers. Within 48 hours, all the children had clear skin. The Communist exclaimed, "If you two are any example of what Americans are like, I'm all for America."

Father Ted managed to visit every volunteer and deliver that personal letter from President Kennedy. Waiting for his return plane in the Santiago airport, he sighed with satisfaction.

He pulled out his notebook and read down his list of volunteers, smiling as he remembered the work he had seen each one doing. When he got home, he called all their parents. Some of the volunteers had given him specific messages for their folks, but he let every single one know why they should be proud of their children.

Almost 20 years later, Father Hesburgh once again found himself traveling bumpy roads. It was July, 1980, and he was in the lead Land Rover in a convoy crossing Cambodia. Since there was still fighting going on, two young Vietnamese soldiers with AK-47 rifles were guarding him.

A reporter sharing the truck with him asked, "Don't those guys make you nervous? After all, they are Communists."

"Look," Father Ted shot back, "when someone is hungry, you don't ask him what his political beliefs are, you give him something to eat. I know there's danger involved, but I can't sit back and have it on my conscience that I did nothing to stop a second Holocaust."

"Holocaust?" questioned the reporter, thinking about six million Jews and other "undesirables" the Nazis put to death during World War II. "That's a pretty extreme comparison, isn't it?"

"I don't think so," said Father Ted. "A million Cambodians have had to flee their country to avoid being killed in fierce fighting between rival armies, each bent on controlling the country. A million—many of them orphaned children! They were trapped near the border of Thailand without food, medicine or shelter. Isn't that a Holocaust, an attack on a whole group of people?

"Many of us stood by during that War," he continued. "We later claimed we didn't know the extent of what was going on. We vowed, 'Never again!' But what's taken place in Cambodia is a mass assault on the basic human right to life. We can't say we don't know this, and we can't let this suffering continue." (O'Brien p. 152f.)

"So what did you do when you first heard about all this?" the reporter asked.

"I tried to mobilize people from many nations and religious groups to help. Our National Cambodian Crisis Committee raised half a million dollars, sent volunteers to serve in the refugee camps, and delivered 60,000 tons of seed so Cambodia could survive. We're literally saving a people from extinction."

"Okay, that makes sense," agreed the reporter. "But did you have to come to check on it in person? Bump along over all these miles, stop at all these checkpoints, go without food and water yourself? How old are you anyway, if you don't mind my asking?"

"I'm 63," Father Ted answered. "I had to come see for myself that these supplies are actually getting into the hands of the people who desperately need them. For me, this is a minor, temporary inconvenience. I have so much admiration for the wounded Cambodian people. They're so brave! Look at this! This was once a thriving village. It's been devastated by the war so there's nothing left."

"In the face of all that, don't you feel hopeless sometimes?" the reporter pressed.

"I'm full of hope!" declared Father Ted. "It's great to be able to see a need and be able to do something about it!"

"I take it this isn't just a recent interest," the reporter surmised.

"No, it isn't. Whenever I look into the faces of hungry men, women and children, I understand the premium the good Lord placed on feeding the hungry and giving drink to the thirsty." (O'Brien p. 147)

"You seem to be a very compassionate person."

"Yes, but compassion, alone doesn't get you anywhere,"

Father Ted said. "I mean, I can be compassionate every time I pick up the newspaper and see the AIDS in Africa...and I can bleed for it, but it doesn't really get anything done. The trick is how to turn compassion into action!" (Ifill interview)

He said no more to the reporter, but he couldn't help remembering small ways he had been able to make a difference in other parts of the world. He was appalled by apartheid in South Africa, where black people were systematically excluded from participation in society. He knew he couldn't change that overnight, but he found one small thing he could do. He began sponsoring scholarships so black students from South Africa could attend college in the United States.

Of course he'd also had lots of brainstorms that never came to fruition, like using satellites to help children in remote areas learn to read. He'd always wished college students could receive scholarships for Human Development instead of military service. And he'd love to see the Sinai Desert irrigated using nuclear power so displaced Palestinians could survive there. A diplomat told him that would cost too much. Father Ted asked him if it would cost more than a war.

The reporter broke into his thoughts. "So I guess you really think one person can make a difference in this world."

"Of course I do! The world is full of heroes who made a difference! Martin Luther King, Jr. Albert Schweitzer. Mother Teresa. The list goes on and on. Of course one person can make a difference! And he'll never know how much of a difference he can make until he tries."

Father Hesburgh later wrote, "I have lived long enough to see real, significant changes made for the good...and I have been fortunate enough to have participated in some of them...One person can make a difference!"

Chapter Fourteen

# The Realization of a Very Great Dream

F ather Hesburgh and Pope Paul VI had just finished a simple private dinner in the papal apartment when the waiter came in carrying a large cake. "Wow, that's some cake!" exclaimed Father Ted.

"I've studied and eaten here for three years," he went on, "but I've never seen a cake like that."

Smiling broadly, Pope Paul explained, "It's for you. Happy birthday."

Father Ted was stunned. How did the Holy Father know it was his birthday?

"To your health," said the Pope, raising the glass of champagne the waiter had just filled.

"And to yours," Father Ted replied. "Your Holiness, if you aren't too busy tonight, I brought some of the space movies you love so much."

"Thank you," said Pope Paul. "I'd really enjoy watching them with you."

Partway through one movie, as an astronaut bounced along the surface of the moon, the soundtrack began the Beatles' song "Yellow Submarine." Father Ted glanced over at the Pope, who was grinning and nodding his head in time with the music.

Father Ted whispered, "Your secretary told me watching space movies is the only time you ever relax."

After the films ended, Father Ted asked, "Do you remember when you first visited Notre Dame?"

"That would have been in 1960 for Notre Dame's graduation," the Pope replied.

"I'll never forget how desperate I was," Father Ted recalled. "Less than a month till graduation, and I was batting zero. I had no one to give the commencement address, and no one to celebrate the baccalaureate Mass the day before graduation. I'd asked five Cardinals, and all of them had to say no."

"How did you come up with me?" Pope Paul wanted to know.

"My secretary, Helen Hosinski, knew I was stumped. She said, 'Why not go right to the top and ask President Dwight Eisenhower to be the speaker?' Since we were aiming high, I decided to invite you to celebrate the Mass. Of course, at that point you were Giovanni Battista Montini, Cardinal of Milan, Italy. Little did I know that in only three years you would become Pope Paul VI!"

Father Ted took a sip of champagne before he continued. "I can't tell you how thrilled I was when both you and Eisenhower accepted on such short notice."

"My English wasn't so great at the time," Pope Paul admitted. "I was grateful you could speak Italian." He tapped his fingers together. "I enjoyed that weekend very much."

"We walked all over the Notre Dame campus," Father Ted remembered. "You wanted to stop in every dorm chapel to pray."

"So many lovely places to pray on your campus," the Pope

smiled. "And so many young people praying. It lifted my spirits."

"You brought us many wonderful gifts!" Father Ted remarked. "I especially liked the copies of sketches signed by Leonardo da Vinci."

"A small gift for your hospitality," said the Pope. "Meeting President Eisenhower was also a highlight of the weekend for me."

"I remember that you gave him a small marble statue of an angel holding broken chains," Father Ted recalled. "He was visibly touched when you told him it symbolized what he had done for Europe as commander of the Allied army. Under his leadership, the Allies finally broke the power of Adolf Hitler's Nazi Germany."

"I spoke from my heart when I told him, 'You freed us and we are deeply grateful.'" The Pope bowed his head.

Father Hesburgh's private dinner with the Pope was one of many such occasions. Once Pope Paul gave him a hard time. "Where have you been, my friend?" he asked "I heard you've been in Rome, and you haven't come to see me."

"Holy Father," Father Ted explained, "you are very busy. You know I would come to see you if I had something to talk to you about, but I don't want to just come in and waste your time."

The Pope clapped Father Ted on the shoulder. "Well, I'm telling you that when you are in Rome, I want to see you."

"Then I promise to visit you every time I'm in Rome, Holy Father," Father Ted smiled.

In April, 1963, Pope Paul VI invited Father Ted to stop and see him on his way to Paris. At this time, Vatican Council II was still going on.

A Council is an official gathering of the whole Church, represented by its Bishops. Its task is to understand what

God is saying and doing right now. What a Council teaches and decides shapes how God's Church thinks and acts in the world from that time on.

Pope John XXIII had first convened this major gathering of the world's Bishops and theologians. Although he treasured the rich tradition of the Roman Catholic Church, he felt that being a Catholic should mean more than showing up for Sunday Mass, putting money in the collection basket, and trying not to lie or steal.

When he called the Council, he said, "I want to throw open the windows of the Church so that we can see out and the people can see in." Vatican II (1962-1965) tried to find effective ways to share truth with the modern world. Its documents changed the way the Roman Catholic Church prayed, understood its role, and related to the rest of the world. For example, it encouraged people to participate actively in the Mass they were attending rather than reading individual prayers out of their prayer books while the priest said prayers at the front of church with his back to them. Catholics began to hear readings from many more books of the Bible in their own language. They also prayed parts of the Mass along with the priest and said "Amen" to show they agreed with the words the priest voiced.

Although Vatican II was a Roman Catholic assembly, the Catholic Church invited representatives from other Christian churches and even other world religions to be official observers. This was a radical step, especially since earlier councils were called to defend the Roman Catholic Church against attacks by other churches. Now those very churches were invited to participate.

As usual, Pope Paul VI was happy to see Father Hesburgh. As they walked into the papal gardens, he said, "Congratulations. I understand you've just been elected President of the International Federation of Catholic Universities."

"Thank you, Very Holy Father."

"May I share a dream with you?" asked Pope Paul VI.

"I would consider it a great privilege," Father Ted answered.

"Of course you know that Vatican II has been a wonderful gathering of Roman Catholic theologians and Church leaders. But one of the reasons it's been special for me has been the opportunity to dialogue with leaders from other branches of Christianity—Greek Orthodox, Lutheran, Pentecostal. I've grown to like and respect them very much. I don't want to see that ecumenical cooperation end when the Council is over."

"There's more on your heart, isn't there?" Father Ted prompted.

"Our Lord prayed that we might all be one. I'd love to hasten the day when Christians are no longer divided into separate denominations."

"And your dream?"

"To create a place where theologians from many traditions can live and study together—an Ecumenical Institute."

"Here in Rome?" Father Ted looked out over the city.

"Too Catholic. Geneva, Switzerland, is too Protestant."

"I suppose Canterbury, England, is too Episcopalian and Moscow, Russia, is too Orthodox. How about St. Francis' hometown, Assisi?"

The Holy Father ventured a small smile. "Tempting," he said, "but too romantic."

"What's left?" asked Father Ted.

"The perfect place." The Pope's eyes sparkled. "Jerusalem, where Christianity began."

Then Pope Paul looked Father Ted straight in the eye and said, "I'd like you to take on the responsibility for this ecumenical institute."

Father Ted gulped. "Holy Father, I've been involved in a lot of things in my life, but never with ecumenism. I hardly know anything about it." He paused a moment. "Yet I find your idea very appealing. Tell me more."

The longer they talked, the more willing Father Ted became to take on this new assignment. "What kind of building did you have in mind?" he asked the Pope.

"Something very simple, with a chapel in a central position."

"Yes, I like simple," agreed Father Ted. "What if we had Benedictine monks living there all the time, surrounding and supporting the scholarly work with prayer twenty-four hours a day?"

Pope Paul smiled again. "I like the way you're thinking," he said.

"This is going to mean a great deal of work for you," the Pope continued. "Thank you for serving the Church this way."

After lunch, Pope Paul led Father Ted into his library, where he pulled out an official copy of the very first document of Vatican Council II, on the liturgy. This document changed the celebration of the Mass from Latin to the local language of the people. "I've signed one of these for the Vatican Archives," he said, "and one for my personal archives. Now I am going to sign the third copy for my favorite Catholic university, Notre Dame."

"Thank you, thank you, Very Holy Father," said Father Ted, overwhelmed by the Pope's generosity in giving Notre Dame a Church document of such historical significance. "Notre Dame will treasure it."

As Father Ted strode rapidly across St. Peter's square after this meeting with the Pope, his mind was spinning. His first task was to find a location in Jerusalem for this new institute. He knew Pope Paul VI's representative for Jordan and Jerusalem had already been looking for a year and a half without finding anything.

Before long, Father Ted found himself driving around Jerusalem with his friend Father Pierre Duprey. "Wow!" he exclaimed. "I'd forgotten how much history is packed into so little space!"

"I'm glad we could be here at the same time," said Father Pierre, who normally worked in Africa. "It'll be a fun memory for me."

The two stopped to visit one site after another, but Father Ted shook his head time after time. "Hard to explain why, but this just doesn't feel like the right place."

"I totally agree," said Father Pierre. "Let's get out of the middle of town and gain a little perspective." They drove through the gates and down the hill.

As Father Ted looked back, he could see the old walled city of Jerusalem nestled on top of a high hill. Farther down the hill, they were passing more modern homes and buildings.

Finally they reached a remote hilltop surrounded by olive and pine trees.

"This is Tantur," said Father Pierre.

"Ah," said Father Ted, glancing around at a few deserted buildings that looked like they were once a hospital and a school. They got out of the car and walked around the property. Father Ted ran his hand over an ancient crusader gate and spotted a chapel with thick walls. "Tell me about Tantur," he invited.

"The property covers 35 acres." Father Pierre took him to the top of the hill. "This is the highest point for miles around. If you look that way, you can see Bethlehem, where Jesus was born. Behind you is Jerusalem, where he died."

"Look!" Father Ted pointed west. "You can see all the way to the Mediterranean Sea!" Then he turned east. "Are those Arab villages over there?"

"Yes, they are," said Father Pierre.

"Who owns the property now?" Father Ted wanted to know.

"Some Austrian Knights of Malta developed it a hundred years ago, but they haven't lived here for a long time."

"This is a beautiful location," said Father Ted. "Let's nose around a little more."

Eventually the Catholic Church bought the land from the Knights of Malta. Since Notre Dame was going to run the Ecumenical Institute, the Church then rented the property to Notre Dame for fifty years at a dollar a year.

Father Hesburgh gathered an advisory committee of thirty people who represented all the major Christian churches. Over the next seven years, he traveled a quarter of a million miles to meet with religious leaders all over the world. Together they came up with a wonderful building plan for the site.

The Ecumenical Institute for Advanced Theological Studies opened at Tantur in November, 1971. "What you see here is the realization of a very great dream," Father Ted said.

In 1978 Pope Paul VI died, having seen his dream for an Ecumenical Institute fulfilled.

The next time Father Ted went to Rome, he remembered his promise to Pope Paul VI. Since he could no longer see him in person, he went to pray at his tomb. Laying his hand on the tomb, he promised to stop by and pray there on every visit to Rome.

In subsequent years, thousands of "Protestant, Orthodox, Anglican and Catholic theologians of all ages, both men and women, have lived, studied, and prayed together at the institute. The dream of Pope Paul VI lives on today at Tantur in Jerusalem, working to achieve Christian unity at a place where Christianity began," wrote Father Hesburgh in his autobiography. Jewish and Muslim scholars have also spent time at Tantur.

Father Hesburgh expresses his conviction. "You have to hope that in our times the Muslims and the Christians and the Jews somehow learn to get along together...There is no reason why we should be fighting each other, because we all believe in one God. We believe in a loving God, in an understanding God, in a forgiving God and a blessing God. And for us not to get along is terrible." (Hunnicutt p. 15)

Chapter Fifteen

# Universities Spinning Out of Control

Sometime after midnight one May evening in 1970, Father Hesburgh heard a noise. He turned down his classical music. Yes, there was the knock again! He hurried to open the tall window and let in a student.

"I saw your office light on," he explained, "so I climbed the fire escape."

"What can I do for you?" Father Ted asked.

"Sir, I have to warn you: some students are probably going to burn down the ROTC building tomorrow."

"And do you support that action?" asked Father Ted.

"No!" he shot back. "I'm student commander of the Army ROTC. I came over because it makes me mad and I thought you should know."

Father Ted didn't ask for names, but the worry lines on his forehead grew even deeper.

"Thank you for coming to tell me," he said. "You're a fine young man. Tell me, how did you become interested in ROTC?"

"To tell you the truth, Father, I really wanted to come to Notre Dame but I couldn't afford the tuition. So I did it for the scholarship."

The student sighed and leaned against the door jamb. "But the more I get into it, the less I care about the scholarship. I've had to pray long and hard about this. I know as soon as I graduate, I'll probably be shipped out to Vietnam. And I have to tell you, Father, my blood runs cold when I watch the news and see all those body bags coming home."

"So what's kept you in the program?" Father Ted asked gently.

"I have to believe I've found something worth giving my life for, if need be. I can't stand by and watch Communism take over the world. The freedom we have here in this country is too precious to me."

"I'll bet other students challenge your commitment," guessed Father Ted.

"They sure do," admitted the student. "The longer this war drags on, the less sense it makes to most people. They say the government of South Vietnam is weak and corrupt. They say we can't beat the North Vietnamese Communists. They use guerilla tactics so you can't even find the enemy."

"This issue raises a lot of passion, doesn't it?" Father Ted observed. "And I can't blame your classmates. The day he turns 18, every young man on this campus has to register for the draft. He's exempt as long as he's in college, but every one of them knows he could be drafted as soon as he graduates and wind up fighting halfway across the world."

"I guess that's why anyone in uniform makes other students scared and angry," said the student.

"So what do you think? Is Notre Dame wrong to have an ROTC program?" asked Father Ted. "Should Notre Dame students be training for war?"

"What do you think, sir?" asked the student.

"As long as nations need armies," said Father Ted, "the United States should have the best Army possible, run by the best people possible. That means people who have thought deeply about God, right and wrong, logic, and history—exactly the subjects we teach best at Notre Dame.

"Of course," he continued, "in the best of all possible worlds there would be no wars, no need for soldiers, but we're not there yet."

"Thank you, Father," said the student. "Your support means a lot. I'd better go. Tomorrow starts early for me."

Father Ted patted him on the shoulder. "I appreciate your coming to warn me," he said.

Father Ted sighed. He went back to work, but soon another student knocked at the same window.

"Father, they're planning a big rally tomorrow afternoon. The organizers have something violent in mind, but they're starting with speeches. They plan to ask you to speak."

"I'd be honored," Father Ted told him.

"Father, you might want to think twice about that," said the student. "They plan to make fun of whatever you say. And look out for rotten tomatoes."

"It's a tough time to be a college president," Father Ted said, pulling a piece of yellow paper out of his pocket. "This is a list of university presidents who've gone down the tubes."

"Gone down the tubes?"

"You know," Father Ted explained, "they've either quit or been fired as a result of student demonstrations. Because I'm president of the Association of American Colleges, I know all of them personally."

"Is it a long list?" asked the student.

"Nearly 200," replied Father Ted. He gave the student a wry smile. "I keep checking to make sure my name isn't on it."

"Well," countered the student, "it's not such a great time to be a college student either."

"I think I know what you mean," said Father Ted. "But I'd like to hear it from you."

The student looked sadly down at his hands. "So much injustice!" he exclaimed. "This war. The way black people and poor people are still being treated. And don't even get me started on all the rules here."

"So do you think students are justified in turning violent?" Father Ted picked up a stack of newspapers and pointed to one headline after another: "100 Students Burn Draft Cards"; "University President Barred from Office, Blood Poured on Rug." Wearily he put down the stack. "Feels to me like universities all over the country are spinning out of control."

"So are the people in charge!" the student shot back. "Do you think police should be clubbing and shooting students?"

Father Ted shook his head sadly. Only a few days earlier, Ohio National Guard troops had fired into a crowd, killing four Kent State University students. "No wonder everyone's upset," he said.

"I'll let you get back to work, Father," said the student. "I just wanted to warn you."

"I thank you," said Father Ted, ushering him to the door.

After the student left, he glanced up at a picture on his office wall. In it, his arms were linked with Dr. Martin Luther King and other civil rights marchers singing "We Shall Overcome." He remembered his grief the day Dr. King was assassinated.

So many senseless deaths in such a short time! In 1963, President Kennedy was shot in a motorcade in Dallas, Texas. Five years later, it was his brother Bobby, campaigning for President. Those three assassinations felt like direct attacks on the ideals of justice and equality that meant so much to Father Hesburgh and the college students he knew and loved.

Yes, he understood why young people were disillusioned. He was as keenly aware of tragedies and injustices as they. But there was an important difference. He knew from experience that real change often took a long time. And he knew that students often chose the wrong way to get what they wanted.

He remembered a reporter asking him, "What's the matter with this generation?"

"What's so good about you or your world?" Father Ted countered. "Is there nothing to be uneasy about, nothing to protest, nothing to revolt against? We might begin by trying to understand what causes the unrest, the protest, the revolt of the young people today."

His mind went back to March of 1969. Students from several different groups invited Father Hesburgh to meet with them. They told him that despite their different ideas and approaches, they all agreed on one practical thing: the university should promote the study of non-violence through courses, talks and a special library collection.

"What a great idea!" he told them. "But I'm sure you realize putting together a program like that would take a lot of work and cost a lot of money. It's not going to happen overnight. How about this? You work on finding teachers willing to do the work, and I'll start looking for the money."

The next afternoon, Father Ted's phone rang. A reporter from the student newspaper wanted to make sure he had his story right.

"You said you'd take care of the money, right? What I need to know, then, is how long it's going to take you to get it—six days, six weeks, or six months after we're dead?"

Father Ted said, "I already have the money!" There was a stunned silence on the other end of the line.

"I can't believe my ears," said the student as he hung up.

Father Ted chuckled. He thought of one of his favorite sayings, "The one thing we really know about tomorrow is that the providence of God will be up before dawn."

Earlier that very day the vice president of Gulf Oil flew in to meet with Father Hesburgh, who had no idea why the executive wanted to see him. He soon found out.

"Gulf Oil wants to donate $100,000 to Notre Dame," the executive announced. "What's the college's greatest need?"

Father Ted got goose bumps. He sketched the students' proposal for the study of non-violence. There was a long pause while the executive mulled it over.

"We weren't thinking about anything like this," he said slowly, "but it seems to me you're making a move Gulf Oil would be proud to be a part of." By the time he left, Father Ted was holding a check for $100,000.

When his telephone rang in the wee hours of that long night, Father Ted snapped back to the present. Just as he expected, the student body president said, "Oh, Father, we're going to have a big rally out on the main mall at one or two tomorrow afternoon, and we thought maybe you'd like to speak."

Without hesitation, Father Ted said, "Thank you. Of course I would."

Thoughtfully he hung up the phone. He leaned his head on his hands and prayed about what to say to the students the following day. He was used to speaking to all kinds of groups without notes, but this time he knew he had to choose every word carefully.

He pulled out a sheet of paper and began writing. Near dawn, he left the talk for secretary Helen Hosinski to type and crawled into bed for a few hours.

The next day, Father Ted looked out over a crowd of 2,000 students gathered on the lawn. Some were curious, others downright hostile. He spotted the students who had climbed his fire escape the previous night.

"Thank you so much for inviting me to speak," he began. "I can't tell you how much I admire your strong convictions.

"You all know that I strongly supported America's role in World War II," he said. A murmur of disapproval ran through the crowd. "However," he continued, "were I in a position to do so, I would end this war tonight before midnight." He listed some practical suggestions for the President of the United States: get out of Vietnam, end the draft, and give people the right to vote when they were 18 instead of 21.

A few students clapped, and then the applause became a wave. They liked his talk so much that they never picked up those tomatoes. Instead, they went door to door asking the people of South Bend to sign copies of the speech. Then Father Hesburgh sent President Nixon 23,000 signed copies.

Even though the rally on the lawn ended well for Father Ted, there were still students who wanted to burn down the ROTC building. Soon after his speech, all the different student groups sponsored an all-night meeting about setting fire to the ROTC building. They agreed to listen respectfully to everyone who wished to speak, and then put it to a vote. They would abide by what the majority wanted.

The meeting went on for hours as students and professors voiced strong opinions on both sides. Finally it was time to vote. Since a large majority voted against torching the building, that was the end of the matter.

However, it was not the end of student discontent and anger. Besides national and international issues, students chafed at rules that hadn't changed since their parents were in school. How could Notre Dame treat them like children when they were old enough to die for their country? They flaunted rules about everything from hairstyles to curfew (the time you had to be in your dorm). For example, one Notre Dame student wore a tie to the dining hall as required, but the dress code didn't mention a shirt, so he came without one. These rules seemed trivial to students, but Father Ted knew what they were for—to create a civilized culture in which learning could take place. There was no place for alcohol or drugs in such a culture.

Again and again, student leaders sought meetings with the president, asking him to give in to specific demands. They wanted permission to entertain girls in their rooms. They wanted a specific quota for minorities in the student body. They wanted to show pornographic movies at Notre Dame. They wanted students to be involved in university decision-making.

Father Hesburgh listened respectfully to every concern, but he also defended university policies. Although he was grateful to the students who climbed the fire escape to let him know about the anti-war rally, he was not always so kind to unexpected visitors.

In the wee hours of another morning, he looked up from a phone call and saw a student standing in front of his desk, taking a swig out of a can of beer. "I want to talk to you," he demanded.

Father Ted put his hand over the receiver. "I have exactly four points to make. One, you are never to walk into my office without knocking. Two, it is not polite to listen in on another person's conversation. Three, it's against the rules to drink beer on campus. Four, get back out in the hall until I am finished with my call. After that, if I've cooled off sufficiently, I may come out and talk to you."

Dissatisfied students continued to organize one protest after another. Father Ted talked it over with Father Ned.

"How can I help them understand the difference between

free speech and actions that interfere with the rights of others to teach, learn or pursue unpopular goals?"

"Why don't you put your policy in writing?" Father Joyce suggested. "Draw a clear line, then say exactly what will happen if a student steps over it."

"I like that," said Father Ted. "I'm going to start drafting it right away. Furthermore, I'd like to get every part of the university community to agree before I publish the policy."

Father Hesburgh wrote a letter to each person on campus, later known as the "Cease and desist" letter. He explained what actions were unacceptable and what would happen if a person refused to stop.

For several months, things were more peaceful, but then companies began visiting campus to interview graduating seniors for jobs. The university scheduled interviews with the CIA and Dow Chemical on the same day, both companies highly unpopular for their role in the war. Since Dow manufactured napalm used to make chemical bombs, a group of students decided to lie down in front of a door, forcing those who wanted job interviews to step over them.

This clearly broke Father Ted's rules. He called the dean of students.

"Jim, I want to be sure the protesters understand they're violating university policy and what will happen if they don't get up. But give them enough time to do the right thing."

Dean Riehle hurried to the scene of the lie-in. He read the protesters the rules and asked them to spend fifteen minutes thinking over their actions.

When he came back twenty minutes later, the students were still stretched out on the floor blocking the office door. The dean picked up their student ID cards and told them they were suspended. He said he planned to leave again for five minutes. Anyone who was still there when he returned would be permanently expelled, never able to enroll at Notre Dame again.

By the time the dean came back, the students had cleared the pathway. They weren't expelled, but they were still suspended for the rest of that semester.

Father Ted was delighted when every one of them returned the following semester and graduated from Notre Dame. He presided over that commencement as usual. No tomatoes were thrown while he was at the podium, and his name stayed off his "gone-down-the-tubes" list.

### Chapter Sixteen

# A Roller Coaster
# Ride I'll Never Forget

"Father Hesburgh, if there is anything I can ever do for you, let me know," U.S. President Jimmy Carter invited.

Father Ted had just finished some special projects for the President. As they met privately in the Oval Office, he congratulated Carter.

"I heard you got a chance to take over the controls recently on a sub making a deep dive."

President Carter grinned. "You know how much that meant to me as a retired Naval officer."

"Well, then," Father Ted said, "I'm sure you can understand what I'm going to ask you to do for me. I've always wanted to break the speed record in an airplane."

"Go on," President Carter urged.

Father Ted cleared his throat. "I know that the speed of sound is called Mach 1. Mach 2 is two times the speed of sound. The world record is 2,193 miles per hour. That's 3.35 Mach, more than three times the speed of sound. If a plane traveled much faster than that, friction would burn it up. I'd like to chase that record."

President Carter smiled. "Only one plane can do that. Of course you're talking about the SR-71."

"You guessed it, Mr. President."

In his low, slow voice, the President said, "She's a beautiful supersonic spy plane. They nicknamed her Blackbird because her special black paint absorbs radar. Instead of weapons, she carries photographic and electronic gear to gather military intelligence—from 80,000 feet up."

President Carter shook his head. "They don't even let civilians see that plane, much less ride in it."

"I know," said Father Hesburgh, "but you're the Commander-in-Chief, so you can order it if you want to."

Two days later, the Air Force chief of staff called Father Ted. "The boss tells me you want to fly in the SR-71."

"It's been my dream since the first time I read about her," Father Ted confessed.

"Well, there are some conditions. First, you have to pass the same physical and psychological tests we put astronauts through."

"That's fair," an excited Father Ted agreed.

"Second, you have to know how to eject from an altitude of over eighty thousand feet. Third, you've got to know how to operate everything in the backseat, on command from the pilot in the front seat—seven radios, a transponder, and navigational equipment."

Undeterred, Father Hesburgh said, "Thanks, I'm looking forward to this." He smiled so much that day that several people asked him what he was so excited about.

A few days later an Air Force major met Father Ted in Chicago to accompany him to Beale Air Force Base outside Sacramento, California.

"I'm glad to meet you," said Father Ted. "I read you flew

the backseat for the SR-71's record-setting flight. Since that will be my position, I'm ready to learn all you can teach me!" Throughout the flight, the two men pored over the manuals for the SR-71.

At Beale, Father Ted went through the same grueling physical and psychological tests astronauts have to take. Even though he was 61 years old, he passed with flying colors. Then he spent three long days learning everything he would need to know about copiloting the Blackbird.

"Come on," his instructor directed. "Let's see how fast you can put on your space suit." He got into it then screwed the helmet onto a metal ring in its collar. He pushed his feet into heavy boots, and pulled thick gloves over his hands.

When every single part of his body was covered, Father Ted wondered how he could push the right buttons on the instruments wearing those bulky gloves. Since he'd be sitting over nine different explosives, he knew he couldn't afford to make a mistake.

His teachers put Father Ted through all kinds of tests to make sure he wouldn't panic under difficult circumstances. One day, dressed in a space suit with an oxygen mask, he crawled into a pressurized tank. Instructors left after they made sure he was bolted into the backseat, but a doctor looked in through the window and monitored his vital signs as they gradually reduced the air pressure to what he would experience 85,000 feet up.

Suddenly a light started flashing. Father Ted didn't know whether there was a real emergency or they were just testing him, but he knew he had to push the "eject" button. In an actual flight, that would shoot him out of the plane faster than a rifle bullet.

Immediately another emergency light began flashing.

That meant there was something wrong with the automatic eject system. He managed to push the right buttons and pull the right handles to do those three steps by hand.

Next he was instructed to push up his visor, cutting off his oxygen supply. He felt like gulping in air, but he knew he should breathe as slowly and shallowly as he could. He'd been breathing pure oxygen for three hours, so his blood contained plenty of oxygen if he didn't panic.

After a minute the doctor asked, "Are your fingers and toes starting to tingle?"

"No, not particularly," Father Ted answered.

"Then go another minute," he directed.

Father Ted went without air for a second and then a third minute. Finally the doctor said, "Count to ten, and back again." This time Father Ted counted as fast as he could.

Finally he heard the doctor say, "That's it. Pull your visor down."

Father Ted took a deep breath. He could feel the oxygen rushing through his bloodstream.

The night before the flight, Father Hesburgh had dinner with the pilot, Major Tom Allison, and his family. "Well, Father Ted, you've passed all our tests. That's quite a feat at age 61."

"I had my heart set on it," said Father Ted, "I'll never forget this experience. And I'll keep you and your lovely family in my daily prayers."

"Father Ted," Tom told him, "Astronauts on a mission like ours get a special breakfast—steak and eggs. Sound good to you?"

"Sounds great," answered Father Ted, "but tomorrow is Ash Wednesday, when Catholics are supposed to fast. That means skipping meat and eating only one full meal."

"Wouldn't the Church allow an astronaut the traditional breakfast, even on Ash Wednesday?" asked Tom.

"I'm sure that would be fine, but I'd rather have just toast and coffee, if you don't mind," answered Father Ted.

"Then I'll join you in fasting," declared Major Allison.

After struggling into his space suit, Father Hesburgh breathed pure oxygen for two hours to build it up in his bloodstream. Near the end of that time, a corporal came in with some bad news.

"I apologize, sir. While I was pulling the pins on your parachute pack, one slipped through my fingers and fell down to the bottom of the plane."

"That doesn't sound too serious," Father Ted replied.

"On the contrary. We don't dare leave it down there. It could rattle around and interfere with sensitive electronic equipment. We'll have to remove the seat and all the explosives, get down there and get it out."

"How long will that take?" Father Ted asked.

"I'm afraid you're going to have to wait about three more hours."

Father Ted winced. Then he realized he'd already waited years for an opportunity like this. He could wait three more hours! And he certainly didn't want this young man to feel any worse than he already felt for dropping that pin.

"Don't worry; it could happen to anyone," he assured the corporal. "But when you find that pin, can I have it as a souvenir?"

Finally Tom and Father Hesburgh climbed into the SR-71 and checked everything one more time. At last Tom said, "OK, we're ready to roll."

Father Ted recalls "And did we ever roll. Tom turned on the afterburners and I felt like someone had just kicked me in the rear. Flames shot out five or ten feet behind each one of those big J-58 engines. About halfway down the ten-thousand-foot runway, we took off like a rocket going straight up. We got to thirty thousand feet in what seemed like only seconds. It was the closest thing to being shot out of a cannon."

Impatient because ground control told them to cruise at "only" .9 Mach, Father Hesburgh asked why. Tom explained, "We're passing over a ski slope. If we break the sound barrier, that could cause an avalanche."

Soon they were cleared to climb to 60,000 feet. "Padre," the pilot explained, "first I'm going to dive to 25,000 and go through Mach 1. Then we're going straight up."

Father Ted recalls, "That was a roller coaster ride I will never forget....We blasted through Mach 2, then Mach 3. I could feel the flesh on my face pulling against my cheekbones and trying to move around to the back of my head."

Eyes glued on the speedometer, Father Ted saw it pass Mach 3.35.

"Major Tom!" he exulted. "We've done it! You and I have just set a new world speed record!"

"Of course you realize it can't go into the Guinness Book of World Records," Tom reminded him. "We didn't follow all the official protocol for that."

Father Ted pinched himself through his thick space suit. At that speed it would only take 45 minutes to fly from Sacramento to Notre Dame!

Back on the ground at Beale, Father Hesburgh asked Tom, "Did you push that plane as fast as it would go?"

"My God, Padre," Tom answered, "I went within five degrees of burning us up. What more do you want?" They gave Father Ted a small medal and took a photo to commemorate the occasion.

Since he had already passed the astronaut physical, Father Hesburgh put his name on a list of civilians who wanted to go up in the space shuttle. He carefully figured out how to celebrate Mass under weightless conditions.

However, after the Challenger spaceship blew up in January of 1986 with schoolteacher Christa McAuliffe on board, civilian space travel was put on hold. Father Ted was never able to fulfill his dream of saying Mass in outer space, but he tells the story of his roller coaster flight on the Blackbird to anyone who will listen.

Chapter Seventeen

# Each Day
# a Welcome Surprise

"Here they come!" said a gardener, nudging his coworker and pointing. "Whoa, I've never seen them in civvies. No black shirt, no white collar!" Father Ted and Father Ned pushed through a hundred well-wishers surrounding an RV with a car attached to its tow-line.

"Hey, Father Ted," the groundskeeper called out. "We're going to miss you guys around here."

"Thanks," Father Ted responded. "I'm sure you'll keep things looking ship-shape as always."

"Take care of yourselves," said another worker.

Father Ted winked an eye. "I'll try, but my own sisters aren't sure I can handle my own laundry and cooking after being spoiled by maids and secretaries for so long."

"When will you be back?" asked a professor.

Father Ted smiled. "In seven weeks we'll fly back for the International Special Olympics Games. It's great to have Notre Dame hosting the games this year, and I wouldn't miss offering the opening prayer for anything. But then we'll take off again for the rest of the summer."

"Hey," one of the onlookers ribbed them. "Are you sure you guys can make it as far as Gary?"

Another called, "Got your maps?"

"Gary's only 75 miles on the interstate," retorted Father Ned. "We're going to put thousands of miles on this spankin' new RV. One of Notre Dame's trustees, Art Decio, is CEO of Skyline Corporation. I'm sure he's equipped this baby with everything we could possibly need."

Notre Dame Athletic Director Gene Corrigan pulled out a bottle of champagne. "What are you going to name her?"

Father Ted said, "We've decided on Lindy. That's Art's daughter's name, but it just happens to be the nickname of Charles Lindbergh, one of my all-time heroes. I was ten the year he flew nonstop to Europe, and he gave me the itch to fly."

Gene crashed the champagne bottle over the bumper while Father Ted said a little prayer.

He stifled a yawn. "Ned, it must have been your idea to get going so early in the morning," he griped.

"You think 9:15 is early?" Father Ned teased. "Guess I'd better drive for the first leg." He climbed into the driver's seat.

Father Ted patted the side of the vehicle. He climbed into the passenger seat and rolled down the window to wave goodbye. To cheers from the crowd, they headed for the back gate out of campus. He leaned over to display a hand-lettered sign, "GARY OR BUST."

Father Ted opened his journal and recorded the date: Thursday, June 11, 1987.

"Can't believe we've actually retired from our command posts," he said. "We insist that our professors take a year off every seven years, but you and I haven't had a sabbatical in 35 long years of very demanding service. We may have had to wait till we were 70, but by golly, we're going to enjoy this."

"Who had this brilliant idea of traveling across the whole western United States in an RV?" asked Father Ned. They both shook their heads. Neither could remember.

"In any event, I need to get far enough away to give Father Ed Malloy the freedom to develop his own style as president."

"By all accounts, he's up to the challenge," remarked Father Ned.

The two friends spent the next three months touring the American West. They were awed by the spectacular scenery and enjoyed the wildlife. One morning in Jackson, Wyoming, Father Ted was startled awake at 3:30 a.m. He sat up in bed looking around the room then started laughing. Three moose were rubbing their noses against the window.

"It is not time for me to get out of bed yet!" he protested. "Especially since we stayed up till 1:30 chatting with our hosts. Say, did Father Ned send you? He's an early riser too."

Near sunset on another day he felt overwhelmed as he looked at the rock formations in Zion National Park. He'd visited about 145 countries on earth and seen most of the natural wonders of the world, but he'd never seen anything more beautiful than this!

Twenty miles outside of Denver, they heard an explosion under the hood and the RV sputtered to a sudden stop. They were barely able to coast to the shoulder, and the RV had to be towed back to Denver. After the mechanics diagnosed a wiring problem, the two priests pitched in to help with the repairs.

Father Ted changed the oil, then he lifted up his hands and looked at them.

"Sure enough, there's grease under my fingernails again," he exclaimed. "You know I used to work in a gas station when I was in high school."

"Do we have something to cook up if we get stranded here?" Father Ned asked.

Father Ted nodded. "Sure; there's steak in the freezer, and I spotted a market in the middle of town selling corn. We always manage fine."

"Well, yes we do, but I'm glad we haven't had to cook very often," Father Ned admitted, "thanks to the Notre Dame alumni wherever we've gone. Lucky for us they're always happy to offer us meals and a place to sleep."

A week later their battery died in Vail, Colorado. Another mechanic had to blow out their gas line and tighten a gasket. But before they could be on their way again, he told them he had to spend 40 minutes recharging the battery.

"No matter," Father Ted assured him. "We're not on a tight schedule."

He conveyed the message to Father Ned. "Guess we'll be here longer than we thought. That gives me time to switch a load of laundry at the laundromat."

"I'll just go mail these postcards," said Father Ned.

Father Ted also stopped in a camera store.

"My camera doesn't seem to be working," he confessed, handing it over.

"Here you go," said the clerk. "You just had the batteries in wrong."

"Whoops. I've always said that I want to learn something new every day. Thanks."

Crossing into Canada, the customs official began giving them a hard time. "What's in that RV?" he asked. "You're going to have to unlock it so I can inspect the contents."

Then he took a closer look at Father Ted and asked, "What's your name?"

"Father Ted Hesburgh."

"I thought you looked familiar. Will you give me your

autograph?" Father Ted scribbled his name on a piece of paper, and the officer waved them across the border.

They were glad they made that side trip. After seeing more breathtakingly beautiful scenery in Canada, Father Ted struck up a conversation with two hotel waitresses. They had been away from the Catholic Church for years but decided to reconsider. One of them ended the conversation by saying, "I guess the good Lord sent you around to talk to me tonight."

After the Special Olympics games, the two priests flew to Alaska for ten days. As usual, Father Ted caught the biggest fish, a 35-pound salmon.

At the end of that long summer, the two priests pointed their RV back toward Notre Dame.

"Have you kept track of our mileage?" Father Ted asked.

"If you count our flight to Alaska after the Special Olympics games, we've covered 18,242 miles," said Father Ned.

Father Ted whistled. "That's a powerful lot of miles," he said, "especially since we did most of it on land. When we got on that plane to fly back to Notre Dame after seven weeks, it was by far my longest spell without a flight in almost forty years.

"I have to admit I'll be glad to get back to Notre Dame," he continued. "It will probably take a month just to catch up on my mail. Are you sure we can make it before the fall semester begins?"

"Relax," said Father Ned. "I know you're eager to greet the students coming to enroll in the new international peace studies program."

Father Ted barely had time to unpack before he was welcoming those students, many in their native languages—Russian, Chinese, Japanese, French, Hindi. He was grateful for Joan Kroc's pledge of $6 million to build the Hesburgh Center for International Studies. Despite Father Ted's protests, she insisted the building bear his name.

Before the end of September, the two friends were off again, this time for a trip through Central and South America. They took in all the tourist attractions from the Aztec pyramids to the mountains of Peru. But Father Ted always had the bigger picture in mind. Besides seeing the sights, they met with local leaders to talk about government, finances, education and poverty in Latin America. They visited many colleges.

Wherever they went, Father Ted reached out to individuals. In Mexico City, he dusted off the prayer for pregnant women he had found so effective when he was chaplain of Vetville.

As they had in the RV, the two priests also managed to say Mass at least once a day. In Cuzco, Peru, Father Ted invited the cleaning ladies at the hotel to join them. After Mass, he noticed one lingering in the chapel, so he went over to her.

"How can I help you?" he asked in Spanish. She wound up seeking his advice about her troubled marriage.

Their travel through Latin America was mostly by airplane, but included cruising Chile's fjords on the *Evangelista*, and taking a one-month trip down the Amazon on the *Society Explorer*.

At several points they disembarked to explore native villages. Cuxin Mini had a lovely chapel but hadn't seen a priest in years. When he learned this, Father Ted went back to the boat to get his Mass kit so he could celebrate with the excited villagers before the boat left at midnight.

Shortly after the end of their Latin American tour, Father Ted and Father Ned found themselves walking up the gangplank of the *Queen Elizabeth II*.

"Wow!" remarked Father Ned. "I didn't realize how big this cruise ship was until we actually saw her. I don't think it will have any trouble getting us around the world."

Father Ted said, "Just think, we start here in the Caribbean, for a Christmas tour. A week or so off, then we'll head through the Panama Canal to Asia and Africa, with stops in Tahiti, New Zealand, Australia, Kenya, India, Malaysia, China, Korea, Japan and Hawaii. 100 days on the high seas. Who could ask for more?"

Father Ned whistled. "You know, I never expected to join you on a trip like this. I was always the one who stayed home and kept everything running smoothly while you gallivanted around."

"I'm so happy to have you along," smiled Father Ted. "I'll have to make sure you find out how it's done."

True to his word, Father Ted hauled Father Ned up on deck one day. "Aw," objected Father Joyce, "We aren't due in Tahiti till Tuesday, and I'm in the middle of a good book."

"It can wait. The *Queen Elizabeth II* is about to cross the Equator. You know, that imaginary line dividing the northern and southern hemispheres," explained Father Ted with mock seriousness. "It's a big deal, so it requires a few festivities. You won't officially become a Shellback unless you come and watch."

"A what?" asked Father Ned.

"Right now, you're a Pollywog. That's someone who's never sailed across the Equator."

"So what's the big deal?" Father Ned persisted. "You must have crossed the Equator by boat at least twenty times!"

"Maybe so," agreed Father Ted, "but this time I can thoroughly enjoy it. I have no responsibilities back at Notre Dame to worry about!"

As passengers lined the railings, the crew was marched out on deck under guard. They were presented to "King Neptune" (god of the sea) and his "Queen," ordered to kiss a dead fish, and doused with ketchup, mustard, eggs and whipped cream.

Finally they were shoved into plastic chairs and dumped into the ship's pool. Laughing, the passengers clapped until the last crew member clambered out of the pool.

"Wasn't that fun, Shellback?" Father Ted asked. Father Ned grinned appreciatively.

"Well, you can get back to your book," said Father Ted. "And I need to polish my homily for Mass in an hour."

Father Ned nodded. "After all, we are earning our way on this cruise by being chaplains."

"Father Ted," a passenger told him, "You've made this cruise almost as good as a retreat for me."

"Thank you."

Another day Father Ted was walking on deck with a passenger. "Your homily on marriage today was one of the best I've ever heard!" he exclaimed. "Hmm," said Father Ted. "I have to give the Holy Spirit all the credit for that one. You see, I got mixed up and prepared a homily for the Feast of St. Paul. I didn't realize that feast is tomorrow until I re-checked the lectionary. So what I said about marriage was entirely off-the-cuff."

"Well, it hit me between the eyes. In fact, I was wondering if I might talk with you about my own marriage."

"Sure," agreed Father Ted. "Let's find a couple of deck chairs."

When the two priests were walking to dinner, Father Ted said, "You know, there are several cancer patients on this cruise who don't have many more weeks to live. How I admire their attitude!"

"Is that why you preach on fearlessly looking forward to death with great anticipation and wonderment?" Father Ned asked. "And encourage everyone to be at peace with God and himself, and to live each day to the fullest?"

Father Ted nodded. "I only hope when my life is drawing to a close, I can be as courageous as these folks."

Father Ted saw miracles of grace, even in the middle of the ocean.

One day a man in sick bay asked Father Ted to hear his confession. After he poured out his heart and received a blessing, Father Ted turned to leave.

"By the way," the man said, "I'm not Catholic."

Father Ted raised his eyebrows. "You may not be a Catholic," he replied, "but you've just had all your sins forgiven."

On a hydrofoil ride back to Hong Kong from the island of Macao, Father Ted met a young Chinese girl. She turned to him and honestly asked, "What does it mean to be a Christian?" Everything he said was brand new to her!

On each leg of the cruise, there were celebrity guests, ranging from scientists to movie stars. After viewing a solar eclipse under cloudless skies, Father Ted took part in a panel discussion with three scientists about science and religion. The other panelists weren't at all sure they even believed in God, but all four discussed the meaning of life and the possibility of life on other planets.

Toward the end of their world cruise in April of 1988, Father Ned found his friend in the library paging through *National Geographic* magazines.

"No time to start another 800-page book?" Father Ned teased.

"Life is too short," sighed Father Ted. "I'm afraid I may have to visit some ports through photographs."

However, another invitation soon came their way, this time for a Christmas cruise to Antarctica, again on the *Society Explorer*.

"What do you think?" Father Ted asked.

"Well, you've got me hooked on traveling now," admitted Father Ned. "As a southerner, I'm fascinated by snow and ice. But you've already been to Antarctica."

"I was there briefly in 1963," recalled Father Ted, "but this cruise is to the half of the continent I've never laid eyes on. Let's do it."

And so they had one more adventure, a two-week cruise in the land where the midnight sun dazzled on icy landscapes, filling their eyes with icebergs, volcanic mountains and crevasses, penguins and whales of every variety.

Once again the two priests served as chaplains. Once again, they reached out to their shipmates and all they encountered on shore. After paddling to shore in rubber zodiacs, they were able to celebrate Christmas Mass in several languages at science stations whose staffs hadn't seen a priest in months. In the Falklands, Father Ted met a priest from the very town in Tyrol where he had spent his summers when he was a seminarian in Rome fifty years earlier.

At 5:30 a.m. on December 30, 1988, the two priests got off the plane that had brought them from Santiago, Chile, to Miami.

"Well, buddy," said Father Ned, "it sure has been fun traveling the world with you!"

Father Ted grinned. "I agree. Let's hope the rest of our retirement follows this great start—a totally different experience with new and unusual scenes and people, each day a welcome surprise."

### Chapter Eighteen

# I'd Rather
# Wear Out Than Rust Out

"Good morning, Helen. How good to see your smiling face."

"How do you like your new office?" his secretary asked. "I think you'll find all your books and mementoes here."

"It's exactly as I imagined it." Father Ted picked out a book from the floor-to-ceiling bookcases that lined the walls of his office on the 13th floor of Notre Dame's Hesburgh Memorial Library. *Life in the Afternoon: Good Ways of Growing Older.* Yes, there was the signature of its author, Notre Dame professor emeritus Ed Fischer. Father Hesburgh had read the new book during his cruise.

He strode over to the window that covered the west side of his office. "I feel like I've moved up in the world," he remarked. Across campus he could see Sacred Heart Church and the Golden Dome of the administration building. As President of Notre Dame, he'd spent many hours in his office under that Dome.

"You'll be able to keep up with all the new construction from up here," Helen pointed out. She looked sharply at Father Ted. "You seem out of breath," she observed.

"I'm fine," he replied. "I just took the elevator to the eighth floor and walked up the other five flights. It's exactly 100 steps."

"Guess I don't have to worry about your getting enough exercise," she commented.

Father Ted turned away from the window and headed toward the door. "Before I get started on my pile, I'd like to see what Ned is up to."

"His office is right next door," Helen reassured him, "and he came in to work early this morning, as usual."

"Well, you know better than to expect me much before noon."

"I know," smiled Helen. "I've put your correspondence on your desk for you."

"Thank you," said Father Ted. "You did a superb job of taking care of things while I was traveling."

"Ned," said Father Ted from the doorway, "is your golf handicap improving?"

They both laughed. "I can't count how many people have asked me that." Father Joyce slid a file aside. "I'm glad we stayed away as long as we did and gave Notre Dame's new president some room. But Helen has taken several phone calls from people under the Golden Dome who want our take on decisions the new administration is facing."

Father Ted shook his head. "Father Malloy is in charge now, and I won't second-guess him. These fine young Holy Cross priests are going their own good way, and our comments are unneeded, even if we were of a mind to comment."

"It's good we had time on our cruise to talk about what we want to do during retirement," said Father Ned. "We have a lot of energy left in us if we direct it wisely. "

"You're right." Father Ted sat down in an easy chair. "I plan to do as much as I can, as well as I can, as long as I can, and never complain about the things I can no longer do. I plan to focus on only five goals, but I believe those five can change the world and profoundly affect all of humanity."

"As I remember, world peace was right up there near the top of the list." Father Ned sat down in an easy chair close to Father Ted.

"Yes. We have enough nuclear weapons to destroy the world many times over. After a nuclear war, there won't be any human beings left to have problems."

"I know how gratifying it is to you that graduate students from all over the world come to Notre Dame to study in the Peace Institute you started."

Father Ted nodded. "A highlight for me every fall is getting to know those students. Since I've traveled all over the world, I can usually find a way to connect with each one."

"As I remember, the next two are closely related: human rights and justice throughout the world, and human development in the Third World," Father Ned smiled. "You have always set your sights high, Ted. You've given yourself quite a chunk of work."

"Well, don't forget ecology," Father Ted reminded him. "We have to take better care of the earth God gave us."

"As I recall, ecumenism is on your list," Father Ned said. "You already have a beachhead for that at Tantur."

"Ned, I dream of bringing together all Christians, as well as all the Sons of Abraham—Jews, Christians, and Muslims—who call Jerusalem a holy shrine to the one true God."

Father Ned smiled. "And how long are you in town this time?" he asked.

Father Ted flipped open his pocket calendar. "Well, I have a chance to work on that first priority next week. The Notre Dame Club of Delaware has invited me to Wilmington Wednesday night to talk about the nuclear arms race."

"A quick trip there and back?" he asked.

"Not exactly," Father Ted admitted. "As long as I'm there, I'll address the students at the Catholic high school. I'm sure the seniors who hope to attend Notre Dame will want to meet me."

"That's it?"

"The local TV anchor asked for an interview. Since I have several hours between my time at the high school and that session, I plan to visit the Wilmington Free Library and read to preschoolers."

"Never too early to be recruiting for Notre Dame, eh?" Father Ned teased.

Rising from the chair, Father Ted said, "Helen tells me Creed Black wants me to have lunch with him at the Morris Inn tomorrow. Guess I'd better give him a jingle."

"He's head of the Knight Foundation, isn't he?" asked Father Ned.

Father Ted nodded. The many scandals that year had spurred the formation of a commission on intercollegiate athletics.

"Athletics is not on my list of priorities," he reminded Father Ned. "But I suppose I'll have to see him."

The following day, Creed Black urged Father Ted to co-chair the Knight Commission on College Athletics.

"Creed, I'm retired," Father Ted objected. "Why me?"

"Because everyone respects you. Notre Dame has accomplished what other universities only dream of. You've been able to field excellent teams without compromising your academic standards. You have your priorities straight."

"You're right. I'm very proud of the fact that 99% of our scholarship football students since 1965 have graduated."

"So you'll do it?" asked Black.

Father Ted excused himself. "I just don't have time."

"I thought you cared about the integrity of higher education," Black shot back.

"Of course I do," Father Ted responded.

"Well then, do something about it," urged Black. (O'Brien p. 304)

"I'll pray about it and give you an answer tomorrow," Father Ted agreed.

"I certainly hope you'll say yes. After all, we could change the face of intercollegiate athletics." The two men stood up from the lunch table and shook hands. After praying about it, Father Ted accepted the challenge.

After he got back to his office, he returned a phone call from an old friend who wanted him to go hunting. "I'm sorry," he said, "I just can't set aside a weekend for that any time soon."

"Aw, come on," urged his friend. "You've got to slow down sometime! After all, you are over 70 years old. How can you keep juggling so many big tasks? What's your secret?"

"Same way I've always lived," replied Father Ted. "Do what you're doing flat out, giving it your undivided attention. Don't worry about what you just did. Don't worry about what you have to do tomorrow. The real secret to handling the demands upon you is possessing inner peace, born of prayer, especially to the Holy Spirit."

Father Hesburgh remains busy and active. He still comes into the office every day after Mass and lunch, but he usually leaves by suppertime. Not always to go home, though. Often an individual or an organization invites him to dinner or a meeting. Whether they're business executives, senior citizens or teenagers, he talks in a way they can easily understand.

A group of senior citizens asked Father Ted to give a talk on retirement. As he spoke, he noticed several squirming in their chairs, so Father Ted quickly concluded his remarks. "Too many retired people shut off the lights, lock the door, and vegetate. Others may drink too many martinis or play too much gin rummy. That isn't retirement; it's quitting while still having much to give, much to enjoy, much to love, much living yet to do. I may have retired, but that doesn't mean I've moved to the sidelines. I'd rather wear out than rust out.

"But my life isn't all work and no play," he continued. "I do spend two or three weeks every summer at our Holy Cross property at Land O'Lakes, Wisconsin. I fish, read, write, and listen to classical music. For some reason, I always seem to pull in the biggest fish."

Father Ted leaned forward, warming up to his story. "In 1992 I was casting an orange bucktail with a minnow hooked on behind. Suddenly a 25-pound muskie lunged for my bait. He missed, but his momentum landed him right onto my friend Gerry's lap! While Gerry tried to wrestle the fish to the bottom of the boat, I grabbed his belt from behind to keep him from falling in. Meanwhile, our other friend hefted an oar to stun the fish. Of course the round-bottomed boat began to rock wildly, threatening to dump us all in the lake. We all breathed a sigh of relief when that muskie gave up the ghost."

When he finished his talk with this fish story, the group gave Father Ted a standing ovation.

A steady stream of visitors wants to meet Father Ted and learn from his wisdom. One day while Father Austin Collins, C.S.C., was in Father Ted's office setting up Mass for past presidents of Notre Dame alumni groups, two high school students knocked on the door.

"We're from Florida," they explained, "and we've always wanted to meet Father Hesburgh."

Father Austin waved them in, and soon Father Ted was questioning them about their courses and their interests. "Aim high, and keep working hard," he advised.

"We really want to come to Notre Dame for college," they told him.

Father Ted smiled. "Well, you'll have to accomplish that on your own," he said. "I can't even get the university to accept my relatives if they don't qualify for admission."

Father Ted has the same advice for about 40 Hesburgh Scholars, honors students from Notre Dame High School in Niles, Illinois, who crowd into his office once a year. They all sit on the floor, and he talks to them about the importance of a college education. Then he takes time to ask each one his name and what he hopes to study.

Father Ted cares deeply about the people around him, whether he has just met them or known them for 80 years. Typical was a day when he met Professor Ralph McInerny on his way into the library.

"How's your wife?" Father Ted asked, knowing she was struggling with cancer.

"She's not doing very well," Ralph admitted.

"Come upstairs with me," Father Ted invited. "We'll offer Mass for Connie."

Saying Mass every day remains a high priority for Father Hesburgh. Most often he celebrates a late-morning Mass in the residence he shares with other retired priests, but he also says Mass in his office for alumni groups. Of course he has the standard parts of the Mass memorized, but because of his failing eyesight, he has to rely on another priest to read the prayers particular to each day.

Father Ted is happy to accept other invitations but his superior recently asked the rectors of student dorms to stop asking him to celebrate Mass. Although he loves to do that, a typical Mass at 11 p.m. is just too tiring for him these days. However, he still loves to be invited into freshman discussion classes.

Over the years, Father Hesburgh has served on fifty boards and committees, but today he focuses on the five institutes Notre Dame has developed to address his five top priorities: the Ecumenical Institute for Theological Studies at Tantur, Jerusalem; the Center for International Human Rights; the Helen Kellogg Institute for International Studies; the Institute for International Peace Studies; and the Hank Family Environment Research Center. Father Ted's role has been to discuss programs with the staff and board of directors, and to do fund-raising.

Father Ted enjoys children of all ages. At a recent meal at the Morris Inn, alumni invited him to bless their new grandson. He immediately stood up to make the sign of the cross on the child's forehead. He's honored and happy when asked to baptize babies. However, if the baby doesn't have a saint's name, he'll throw in a "Mary" or "Joseph" to be sure that child has a heavenly protector.

One thing that hasn't changed since he was a young priest is the length of the grace Father Ted offers before meals. One of his favorites is this:

> Father, to those who are hungry, give bread,
> And to those such as we, who have bread,
> Give a hunger for justice. Amen.

Over the years, some projects have demanded less time and attention from Father Ted. However, at age 91 he flew off to Washington, D.C., to a groundbreaking ceremony for the last building on the National Mall, a building for which he helped raise funds. Only steps away from memorials to those who sacrificed their lives in wars, it is a monument to peace.

Because Father Ted's vision is so poor, another priest often accompanies him on such trips. In Washington, D.C., Father Paul Doyle, C.S.C., had an adjoining suite. When the two returned to their room, Father Paul noticed a dark, round object on his pillow. Assuming it was a chocolate, he went over for a closer look and found instead a smooth stone.

"Don't eat that chocolate," he warned Father Ted. Then he read him the little card underneath. "From time immemorial, people have held smooth stones in their hands to help them focus and come to a place of peace. Wishing you a peaceful visit to our national capital."

Father Ted's response was swift. "Well, if you have no faith, I guess anything will do," he remarked.

Recounting this story, Father Paul smiled. "Father Ted is amazing. You just scratch the surface, and wisdom spouts forth."

Father Ted remains actively engaged with the world around him. He served as honorary chairman of a fundraising campaign for a local social service center. He often fires off a letter to the editor or a newspaper opinion piece. He wrote the introduction to a new book about Logan, an organization that has served individuals with disabilities for sixty years.

In the midst of all these demands, does Father Ted ever find time to relax? Of course. He reads a wide variety of books, always his favorite leisure-time activity. He counsels individuals who seek his advice. He writes letters, articles, and his own memories and reflections. He listens to classical music while he rides a stationary bike. He's organized reunions with his O'Grady "foster children" and their families. He tried to learn to speak Chinese, but reluctantly decided he was too old to master yet another language.

Growing older slows everyone down. Although Father Ted's mind remains sharp, he is handicapped by macular degeneration, which has almost completely blinded him. He must depend on others to read to him and to guide his steps when he travels anywhere unfamiliar. A Notre Dame student who is one of his readers told her uncle this is an enjoyable but demanding task.

"I often come to words I don't know," she admitted. "Father Ted always picks up on that. But instead of correcting me, he sends me to the dictionary so I can discover the word's meaning and pronunciation for myself. I have it better than some of his older readers, though. I understand he often invites them to smoke a cigar with him."

Another challenge of aging is having to say goodbye for now to so many close friends and family members. Besides burying all of his sisters, Father Ted celebrated the Mass of the Resurrection in May, 2004, for his closest associate, Father Ned Joyce. Secretary Helen Hosinski has also died, so Father Ted is on his second capable secretary, Melanie Chapleau.

It has been almost 25 years since Father Ted officially retired as President of the University of Notre Dame. Although his office is in the Hesburgh Memorial Library, many current students no longer know who Reverend Theodore M. Hesburgh is. No matter. When he enters the elevator to ride up to his office, he extends his hand and introduces himself to anyone riding along.

At the end of his autobiography, Father Hesburgh summarized his own life for today's young people: "He believed, he hoped, he tried, he failed often enough, but with God's grace, he often accomplished more than he rationally could have dreamed."

# For Further Information

## GENERAL

Coyne, Tom. "Father Ted's Mission and Vision Feted" (*South Bend Tribune*, Wednesday, October 10, 2007)

Hesburgh, Theodore M. *God, Country, Notre Dame* (NY: Doubleday, 1990)

Hesburgh, Theodore M. "A Setback for Educational Civil Rights" (*South Bend Tribune*, March 18, 2010)

Hesburgh, Theodore M. *Travels with Ted and Ned* (New York: Doubleday, 1992)

*The Hesburgh Years, The Observer Special Issue* (Spring, 1987)

Hunnicutt, Jerry. *God, Country, Notre Dame: The Story of Father Ted Hesburgh, C.S.C.* (TV documentary) (Los Angeles: Family Theater Productions, 2004)

Ifill, Gwen. *America's Most Honored* (interview July 12, 2000)

Mueller, Thomas J. and Charlotte Ames. *Commitment, Compassion, Consecration: Inspirational Quotes of Theodore Hesburgh, C.S.C.* (Huntington, IN: Our Sunday Visitor, 1989)

O'Brien, Michael. *Hesburgh, A Biography* (Washington, D.C.: The Catholic University of America Press, 1998)

# HONORS

Congressional Gold Medal (December 9, 1999)
en.wikipedia.org/wiki/Congressional_Gold_Medal
Presidential Medal of Freedom (1964)
betterworldheroes.com/freedom-president/index-Presidential
Medal of Freedom

### Chapter 1
Admiral Richard E. Byrd
en.wikipedia.org/wiki/Richard_Evelyn_Byrd Scroll down
to see pictures.
south-pole.com/p0000107
Larry Gould
geo.lsa.umich.edu/geonews/archive/9512/129502
*Eastwind*
uscg.mil/history/webcutters/Eastwind
uscg.mil/history/webcutters/Icebreaker_Photo_Index.asp
Operation Deep Freeze: en.wikipedia.org/wiki/Operation_
Deep Freeze

### Chapter 3
actors
tyrone_power.com
imdb.com/name?Fredric_March/nm0545298
Most Holy Rosary School
mhrsyr.org
Model T Ford
modelt.ca/background
Teddy Roosevelt on hunting
legendsofamerica.com/we-huntbuffaloroosevelt

### Chapter 4
nd.edu
visit ND
virtual tour

### Chapter 6

World War II
   world-war-2.info
**Chapter 7**
vocation.nd.edu
The Order of Melchisedech ordination ceremony (Ottawa:
   Alfi/Dom Publishing, 1998)
*A Priest's Life: The Calling, The Cost, The Joy* (Word Among Us, 2010)

**Chapter 8**
Vetville
   nd.edu/~adminoff/ulon/acces969/vetville

**Chapter 9**
Frank Leahy, Notre Dame football
   und.com/sports(m-footbl/mtt/leahy_frank00

**Chapter 10**
Rancho Las Cruces
   rancholascruces.com

**Chapter 11**
International Atomic Energy Agency
   answers.com/topic/international_atomic_energy_agency
Peace Studies at Notre Dame Video
   kroc.ned.edu/node/349
   Scroll to bottom of page:
   Click on: Kroc 20th anniversary video

**Chapter 12**
Civil Rights Commission
   en.wikipedia.org/wiki/United_States_Commission_on_
      Civil_Rights
Omnibus Civil Rights Act of 1964
   archives.gov/education/lessons/civil-rights-act
Blacks at Notre Dame
   Fosmoe, Margaret. " '50 Graduate Fondly Recalls ND" (*South
      Bend Tribune*, Thursday, February 26, 2009)
Obama at Notre Dame
   gift of photo: chicagotribune.com/news/nationworld/chi-
      obama-notre-dame-hesburgh
text of speech: chicagotribune.com/news/politics/obama/chi-
      barack-obama-notre-dame-speech

**Chapter 13**

Peace Corps
  peacecorps.gov
**Chapter 14**
 Tantur
  tantur.org

**Chapter 15**
Churney, Linda. *Student Protest in the 1960s* (Yale-New Haven
  Teachers Institute, 2008)
Fosmoe, Margaret. "ND Protest in 1969 Recalled" (*South Bend
  Tribune*, Thursday, November 19, 2009)

**Chapter 16**
 "The Ultimate Spy Plane," *Smithsonian Magazine* (July 2009)
  smithsonianmag.com/arts-culture/The-Object-at-Hand-Stealth-
  Machine

**Chapter 18**
Knight Commission on College Athletics
  en.wikipedia.org/wiki/knight_commission

# Father Theodore Hesburgh, C.S.C.

## ~ *Important Dates* ~

February 2, 1913 – Anne Marie Murphy marries Theodore
   Bernard Hesburgh, Bronx, New York

October, 1915 – Ted's sister Mary Monica is born, Syracuse, New York

May 25, 1917 – Theodore Martin Hesburgh born, Syracuse, New York

1920 – Ted's sister Elizabeth (Betty) Hesburgh is born

1925 – Ted's sister Anne Hesburgh is born

1933 – Ted's brother James (Jimmy) Hesburgh is born

June 24, 1934 – Ted graduates from Holy Rosary High School,
   Syracuse, New York

September 1934 – Enters Congregation of Holy Cross,
   Notre Dame, Indiana

August 6, 1935 – Begins one-year novitiate, Rolling Prairie, Indiana

August 16, 1936 – Takes temporary vows of poverty, chastity, obedience

Summer, 1937 – Sails for Rome, Italy, to attend Gregorian University

1939 – Earns Bachelor of Philosophy degree

May, 1940 – Ordered to leave Italy before Hitler overran Europe

June 24, 1943 – Ordained a priest, Notre Dame, Indiana

May 23, 1945 – Earns S.T.D. (Doctor of Sacred Theology),
   Catholic University, Washington, D.C.

July 5, 1945 – Returns to Notre Dame to teach religion,
   serve as Chaplain to veterans

June, 1949 – Named Executive Vice President,
   University of Notre Dame

June 27, 1952 – Named President, University of Notre Dame (age 35)

1954 – Appointed to National Science Board by President Eisenhower

1957 – Appointed to U.S. Commission on Civil Rights
   (chairman 1969-1972)

1957 – Named Vatican representative, International Atomic
   Energy Agency

1961 – Peace Corps volunteers for Chile trained at Notre Dame

1963 – Trip to Antarctica with National Science Board

1964 – Awarded Medal of Freedom by President Johnson

1967 – Notre Dame turned over to lay board of trustees
(instead of priests)

November, 1971 – Ecumenical Institute opened, Tantur
(Jerusalem), Israel

Fall, 1972 – Notre Dame first admits female students

February 28, 1979 – Breaks speed record in SR-71 spy plane

1979 – Becomes Co-chair, Cambodian Crisis Committee

March, 1982 – Official U.S. observer, elections in El Salvador

1985 – Creates Institute for International Peace Studies at Notre Dame

June 1, 1987 – Retires as President of Notre Dame, leaves on world tour

1990 – Appointed to Knight Commission on Intercollegiate Athletics

July, 2000 – Awarded Congressional Gold Medal by
President Clinton *(approved by Congress December, 1999)*

Cover photo: Father Ted Hesburgh in Antarctica, 1963